# Praise for *No Longer That Girl*

"In Stephanie's compelling memoir she reminds all readers of the possibility of healing and transformation. In this special and specific story we find the universal truth that when secrets are kept, we bear the burden of shame on our backs. When we share that burden, we are free to love that very same world. . . ."

**—Rev. Becca Stevens, founder of Thistle Farms and author of *Practically Divine***

"*No Longer That Girl* shows a young girl's fight to find her voice amid moral confusion and serial betrayals by men in positions of power. Using writing and therapy to help unpack her traumas, the author finds healing by courageously facing her past."

**—Liz Kinchen, MA, Certified Mindfulness Teacher, author of *Light in Bandaged Places***

"Stephanie Maley shares the traumas and lessons of her life with candid courage. Her unflinching storytelling exposes secrets kept in dark corners to protect "polite" company and opens a space for people with similar stories to find relief and affirmation, showing that our worst experiences do not defeat us."

**—Rev. Mary Reynolds Hemmer, author of *Phe and the Work of Death***

"In this powerful memoir, Stephanie opens her heart to share a life filled with resilience, hope, and love. Her story is a reminder that life, though complicated, can still be beautiful. Through her experiences, readers will find strength in their own lives and take away lessons of courage and authenticity."

**—McKenzie Coan, Paralympian gold medalist and author of *Breaking Free***

"A raw and unfailingly honest account of a survivor's long journey home to herself. Maley has written her broken heart whole in these pages and, with powerful authenticity, invites readers to find healing in telling their own truth."

**—Malia Bowers, PhD, Professional Lecturer, Department of Political Science, DePaul University**

# no longer that girl

# no longer that girl

retracing the scars of
the past and present

*a memoir*

Stephanie L. Maley

SHE WRITES PRESS

Published in 2025 by
She Writes Press, an imprint of The Stable Book Group

32 Court Street, Suite 2109
Brooklyn, NY 11201
https://shewritespress.com
Library of Congress Control Number: 2025911506
ISBN: 979-8-89636-008-7
eISBN: 979-8-89636-009-4

Interior Designer: Andrea Reider

Printed in the United States

Names and identifying characteristics have been changed to protect the privacy of certain individuals.

In honor of Mama and in memory
of my goddaughter, Tory

To my husband and sons,
the loves of my life

Girl with warm brown eyes
Bruised soul, hidden wounds cloaking.
She takes up a pen.
Carapace cracks and dissolves
*So she can shine like the moon.*

—R. T. Dake

# PROLOGUE

I need to write my funeral plans. The Covid-19 virus has arrived. Every night I sit on our love seat watching the news. Italians are dying by the thousands. My thoughts churn at the growing numbers of deaths. I walk to my kitchen for water. At the window, I look out, seeing nothing. This virus will kill me. I am a healthy fifty-eight-year-old woman, except when I'm not. Asthma took hold of me when I was twelve years old and hasn't let go. Breast tumors and other health issues find space in my head. There is nowhere to escape from this horror.

My jaw clenches. I must hide from this plague. But how? I don't feel safe in my house. Because my husband is a pediatrician in our small rural community, he spends his day with sick and healthy children and their families. We are aware of how easily the virus could slip into our home since our love binds us so tightly together. The threat from this invisible enemy has pulled my past need to hustle for love to the forefront of my mind and won't let go.

Suddenly, the betrayals and abuse that plagued my early years disturb my thoughts, as if they happened yesterday. I feel so vulnerable again. It isn't as if I never think about them, but now these memories wash over me like an ocean slamming against rocks, coming at me one after another. I want to free my mind.

My present life is so beautiful. My husband, Mike, and I have been married thirty years. We have two sons who are making their way in the world. Both are healthy. Life couldn't be much better—except that my past pops into view like an unwanted ad. I do my best to keep these past traumas from jumping into my mind.

I close my eyes and hope the pain will go away. Instead, deep wounds are bleeding again. I kid myself during the quiet times in my life, thinking those injuries are healed. But, like a nocturnal animal, my earlier life lies in wait, ready to pounce. Covid-19 shines a light on my vulnerability and this beast knows it. There is nowhere for me to run away and hide. Not even therapy helps these days. In the past, it's cleaned and soothed my cuts, but nothing has healed my scars. I want to remove the dark feelings and guilt from my former years, once and for all.

I keep watch and sit with my back to the wall. Hypervigilance is a result of my past. I yearn to stay in the present—to experience each moment as it unfolds without looking over my shoulder each hour of the day.

It is time to live in the present and look to the unknown future. It is time to release the secrets holding me back. My story is begging to be told.

I am slow in finding my voice. Yet time, trust, and therapy together loosen my tongue. Writing this memoir may be my way to slay the beast once and for all.

# CHAPTER 1

*Please look at your phone. Don't abandon me now. I need help. I can't breathe.*

It's March 19, 2020. Panic seizes me. I'm convinced I will die. I sit at my desk, staring at my phone after sending my therapist this text:

"Brooke, I hope you reconsider doing online talk therapy. My anxiety is quite high and talking it out would be helpful. I am terrified of this virus."

I reread what I wrote and realize I am not asking for what I need. I'm not telling her the full extent of what's going on with me.

*Oh my God. I need to write my funeral plans. I am not ready to die.*

A text returns. "Breathe deeply and trust (and focus on) the breath in your lungs. Here's a little reflection for the pandemic quarantine: *And the people stayed home. And read books, and listened, and rested, and exercised, and made art, and played games, and learned new ways of being, and were still. And listened more deeply. Some meditated, some prayed, some danced. Some met their shadows. And the people began to think differently. And the people healed. And in the absence of people living in ignorant, dangerous, mindless, and heartless ways, the earth began to heal. And when the danger passed, and the people joined together again, they grieved their losses, and made new choices, and dreamed new images, and created new ways to live and heal the earth fully, as they had been healed."*

She continues in her text to let me know that this reflection was written many years ago by the Italian journalist Irene Vella.

"Stephanie, go for a walk in the woods with Mike. Listen to the quiet and breathe. Do what you love to do. You're okay."

I fire back what I'm not saying. "I'm afraid I will get this virus and die."

My phone rings. "What's going on?" asks Brooke.

My words tumble out. "I'm going to die. I'm a sitting duck. There isn't anywhere to go to get away from this virus. I've known this, but today I *get* it. Businesses are shutting down. Mike's exposure as a pediatrician makes him a potential coronavirus carrier. And my asthma . . ."

Tears fall down my cheek. My lip quivers as I struggle to catch my breath. My hands twist in my lap. I feel as though I've run a marathon. I see just what's in front of me. News of more deaths and widespread panic fill my computer screen.

"I'm not ready to die. There are so many things I want to do. I'm not protected."

"Let's come up with a plan for you to feel safe," Brooke says, her soothing voice creating a calming balm.

But then the panic returns. "Okay, but I'm a retired nurse and I know how viruses spread. This virus sounds like no other."

"Do you have an anxiety PRN medicine? That might help reduce your anxiety and decrease your feelings of vulnerability."

I take a deep breath and remind her I'm on Lexapro for depression, but not on an "as needed" basis. I have major depressive disorder and I don't want to drop into the pit of it. Fibromyalgia keeps my body in pain most of the time—another thing that weighs me down. As I listen to Brooke's suggestions, my fists unclench. Nail prints mark my hand.

"Ask Mike to put his clothes in the dryer and take a shower when he gets home. He needs to wear a mask and keep six feet away from you. Also, see if you can speak with someone at the Center for Disease Control and Prevention or ask your doctor about your concerns with Mike being a healthcare worker and you feeling vulnerable because of your asthma."

I feel my heart slow down. I call the CDC and sit for an hour and a half on hold, listening to annoying music and announcements, only to talk with someone merely reading the guidelines from their website. I get the runaround from my allergist's office. In the end, Brooke comes up with the plan that eases my panic.

When Mike gets home, we sit across from each other on couches in the den, with Mike wearing a mask. I tell him about my panic and Brooke's suggestions for helping me calm down.

"I've been worried too," he says. "There's so much we don't know."

I lean back on the couch and breathe through my nostrils.

"I'm going to miss being held by you. I'll miss your kisses."

"I will too," he says, "but your safety is more important to me. We're going to get through this."

As with Brooke earlier, sometimes I struggle to ask for what I need. I'm better at protecting others—one of the gifts from my past.

The next morning, I open my eyes and feel the burden of my dreams and the perpetual dread that is present most mornings. The angst that holds me in bed lets loose. Thirty minutes later, I talk myself into getting up. I wash my hair, and my body warms under the showerhead. The goat milk soap slips through my hands. The warm mist opens my nostrils from their allergic, swollen state. I inhale the rich smell as my mind searches for safer times.

I think about our wedding. We were twenty-eight years old and in love. I smile as I remember it and wrap my hair into a turban. I rub exfoliant in my palm and paint my face. The gritty substance makes me look like the Joker. After drying the rest of my body, I remove my long, loose curls from the turban and realize I look even more like the DC comic figure. There are times when I have felt like hiding under a mask.

While my muscles are warm, I bend to touch my toes. My hands hold my body in a downward-dog pose. Fibromyalgia demands that I take the extra time to stretch, and exercising helps me heal from athletic injuries and manage pain. I rinse off the exfoliant and finish my bathroom rituals. These routines help me feel safe and allow my mind to wander.

I remember how Mike's hand was shaking by the time my two fathers delivered me down the aisle and into his care. I snickered and squeezed his hand. Mike found my face and grinned at me. There's nothing shaky about his love for me now, and there never has been.

I dress and greet our small, old dogs who are crated in the kitchen. They sleep upstairs with Mike, then he brings them downstairs in the morning when he leaves for work. I've never slept well with anyone, so I sleep by myself. Mike is an erratic sleeper and needs less sleep. After trying to sleep together for the first three years of our marriage, we resorted to his and her bedrooms. I realize that, with Covid-19, we would need to sleep apart anyway.

"Good morning, good morning, good morning to you," I sing to our Yorkipoos. One of our pups is gray and white with wiry hair. His name is Dusty, and he has the heart of a lion. I recall the pleasure of picking him. He was the runt of the litter but acted like he was tough and independent. This little guy lost his sight a few summers ago and refuses to act any differently.

Rascal, his brother, is black and gray with a white spot on his front right paw. His fur is soft and fluffy. No matter where I go in the house, Rascal stays on my heels. Both of our small dogs are twelve years old. I'm *employed* by these two and don't know what they would do without the five-star attention they receive from me. Of course, they give back to me tenfold in their unconditional love.

I heat a bowl of oatmeal and pray, another one of my morning rituals.

*Thank You, thank You, thank You, thank You, thank You. Help me to listen to Your voice. Teach me to follow Your will. Help me. I lift those in need.*

Tears fill my eyes as I feel the kingdom of God within me. That's the safest place I know. I just need to remember this throughout the day.

I brush my teeth, grab the dogs' leashes, and take Dusty and Rascal for their morning walk. Annie, our outdoor dog, leads the way. She is a mixed breed, covered in white with rust-colored patches. I'm allergic to her dander, so I keep her at arm's length. Somehow, I think she understands.

My blind dog pulls against the leash as the four of us meander down the road. I hear a train in the distance as I search for more happy memories. I need a break from all the Covid-19 news. My body feels tense and strung up. I think of when my birth dad came back into my life.

# CHAPTER 2

"This is from Tom."

"Daddy."

Mama smiles and says, "He's not your daddy. Call him Tom."

She holds a picture of a train. My small fingers brush against the card. She reads the back.

"Dear Stephanie, I saw you wave to me. I love you and will miss you."

"Mommy, Daddy saw me!" I clap my hands together. I'm almost three years old.

One night, before Daddy left on the train, Mommy wasn't in her bed. I like to sneak into her bed, but she always catches me and sends me back to my own bed. When I hurried to find her that night, I got my footed pajamas stuck on the stairs and fell. Mommy and Daddy ran up to me from downstairs. He picked me up and laid me on the rough couch between them. I fell fast asleep. Feeling loved by someone other than Mommy is nice. She has to love me. He doesn't. Daddy comes home and makes everything better. I wish Daddy stayed with us all the time.

When he's with us, I love to press my cheek against him and rub his face with my tiny hands. I love how his arms tighten their grip around my small body. When he kisses me, his soft, warm lips leave a wet spot on my forehead. The world feels so different in his arms. I like feeling wrapped up tight. I want to hold onto him forever. I need him. Mommy seems lost when Daddy isn't with us—so do I. His presence smooths the creases in our family. I want us to be whole like other families. I want to feel safe.

At the end of second grade, Mama and Daddy marry. With my older brother, Brandon, we are finally a family of four. Everything is great.

Six years later, I'm thirteen years old. Anger courses through my blood. I'm about to meet my birth father.

My whole body is tied in knots. My bed and red beanbag chair take a beating from my flopping from one to the other. Footmarks fill my green carpet. If I could unzip my skin and climb out, I would. My chest feels as if I have a jackhammer inside. Like a wounded animal, I remain in my room, hiding from the world.

In the back of my child's mind, I seem to know my birth father, Don, is a doctor. I don't remember how old I was when I overheard my mom tell a friend about him.

"Dr. Corey, Brandon and Steph's pediatrician, won't let me pay for their appointments," Mom shared on the phone. "They knew Don in his residency and that he left us as soon as he was a full-fledged doctor. Brandon was two and Stephanie three months old."

Hearing this conversation also made me aware of money. *If the doctors aren't charging Mom for our visits, then they must feel sorry for us, and my mom needs financial help.* I threw my arms around Mom and hugged her hard. *I won't leave you.*

Since I have never asked about my birth father, this visit was news. Most of the time, Don stayed off my radar. I have my real dad, Tom. My parents didn't talk about him, and I didn't ask. As a young child, sometimes I got random gifts from this unknown man that didn't make sense to me. One time he gave me a blue Samsonite suitcase. I was about eight years old. It looked like something an adult would want. I remember thinking *this guy doesn't know me at all.*

"Come on, Steph," Dad yells up the stairs. "Your father and Joanna are almost here."

This man left me when I was three months old. He is *not* my father.

I peek through my sheer curtains as a car pulls into our driveway. As if on cue, my pulse quickens even more. I lock my door with hunched shoulders and sit on my bed, leaning my head on my fists. I don't want to meet this man. Mom, Dad, and Brandon are outside. Brandon has been excited ever since he heard Don was coming to meet us—of course he is. We have so little in common. I don't want to meet this man, but Brandon can't wait.

*UGH! I figured he was dead. It made sense to me.* His showing up shatters my illusion. *Where has he been? Why now? Do I look like him? I want to disappear.*

Even though I knew I had a birth father out there, he has been like a mirage to me. His coming to see us has blindsided me.

"Stephanie. Get out here now!" Dad is not messing around. "You're being rude."

Don's the one who's rude. Who leaves a baby? Who does that? Why do I have to meet him? I don't have anything to say to him. I hate being made to do this. And why is my dad so set on my meeting Don? I don't care about him. Knowing he's a doctor makes it worse somehow. Doesn't Dad understand how scary this situation is for me? *He's* my dad. I don't need another one! This other man rejected me. I need Dad to protect me.

I drag my feet downstairs and out to the front porch. I feel like throwing up. My muscles feel strung out like a rubber band. Great. He smokes just like my dad. That's probably all they have in common. My dad is handsome with blond hair and blue eyes. This guy is ugly and short—bug-eyed with a Dutch-boy haircut. Bags dangle below his eyes. His wife, Joanna, is the opposite—beautiful with long, black hair. She looks much younger than Don.

A quick glance shows me that the only thing we have in common are brown eyes and hair. I'm just a little shorter than he is, but a normal height for a girl.

*I hate this! I don't want to be polite. How long do I have to pretend to be all happy to meet him? I want him to leave. They want too much from me.*

Mom lifts the Kodak camera to her right eye and takes a photo of the four of us on our front porch. Don leans in my direction while I twist away from him. He holds a cigarette in his left hand. Brandon is on the other side of me with his hands on his hips. I'm half a head taller than Brandon, with an athletic body and long hair. Joanna stands on the other side of Don, looking like a movie star. I do my duty. Done. Check.

"We're at the Read House," Don says. "We'd like to stay a few more days and visit more."

"Let's have dinner tomorrow night," Dad says.

*No. Ask* me *what* I *want.* I feel like giving Brandon to them as a sacrificial lamb, like I hear about in Sunday school. Don and Brandon seem to enjoy each other. They talk and stand close. Brandon has a smile a mile wide. *Fine with me. I want out.*

I imagine a space in my heart where I hide my secrets and pain. I tuck a *Do not trust Don* message in it.

I turn around to go inside. I've never liked this house. I never wanted to move here. Our family's fabric had already started to unravel in our small three-bedroom house in East Ridge, Tennessee. My gut tells me this larger house, with its fancy neighborhood, will undo our family. We connect less frequently. Family dinners are happening less often. Dad doesn't seem happy at home. I picture pieces of thread floating in the air and a wind gust sending them flying in different directions. I feel lost. Now the memory of meeting Don will live on in this disjointed house.

I don't know if I can be polite while Don and Joanna are here. It feels automatic in most situations, but I want to be mean to Don. Anger is burning inside me. I even feel sadness. I've been abandoned and now, because Don decides to see us, I'm supposed to roll over and be all happy. Clenched hands hold my anger. How can my parents want me to be someone I'm not? It feels like I'm choking on a bone.

The next day, Mom finds me in the kitchen.

"We're going to meet Don and Joanna tonight for dinner," Mom says. "Your grandparents are coming too."

We stand in the kitchen. I feel thunder brewing inside me. I snort. Like a bull charging red, my body tenses for battle.

"Do I have to go?"

"Stephie, he won't be here long."

"Long enough already."

"Wear one of your church dresses."

Steam is pouring out of me. "Not a *dress*!"

"Please don't fight with me."

I stomp to my room.

Later, Brandon jumps in the front seat of the car, full of smiles. I cross my arms in the backseat. "Is Dad coming too?" I ask.

"He's going to meet us there," Mom replies.

We pull into the parking lot. My grandparents and Don and Joanna are already here. *I hope Dad gets here soon.*

"Hey Brandon and Stephanie," Don says.

Brandon steps towards him while I take a step back. *Don't even touch me.* Our small parade heads inside.

We're led to a long table in the middle of the room. *Great, front and center.*

Somehow, the only seat available for me is across from Don and Joanna. I can't even look at him. A waitress shows up. Don flirts with her like he's a regular Don Juan. Yuck.

"Steph, what would you like to drink?"

Before I can answer, he asks the waitress if she can make a virgin Cadillac. I make a face.

"I'll talk to the bartender," she says.

He turns to me. "You like sweet drinks, right?"

I nod.

"I think you'll enjoy this one."

I hear a rhumba being played. Couples head to the dance floor. *Where is Dad?*

"I hear you can ballroom dance," Don says.

I ignore him at first, then change my mind. "My dad is one of the best dancers I've ever seen. He's the one who taught me ballroom dancing." Dad owns an Arthur Murray Dance Studio.

I begin to tick off all the things my dad has done for me. "He plays with me and my friends, lets our friends hang out at the house, is my Girl Scout den father. He took us to Disney World just after it opened, he can stay underwater for a long time and took me on a helicopter ride and a small plane." My face feels red. I could go on, but I'm not sure this man cares about what all he's missed.

Don looks at me. I have no idea what he's thinking.

"Would you like to dance?" he asks. I guess that's all he has to offer.

"No." I hear my grandmother make a noise.

The drinks arrive. I take a sip of the Cadillac. It's sweet and tasty. Dang.

Don and Joanna get up to dance. Once they're on the dance floor, Grandmother leans across the table. "Stephie Lee, now don't act like that. Be nice."

"I'm not dancing with him. Look at him. He doesn't know what he's doing. My *dad* knows how to dance."

Brandon seems to be in his own world. He's smiling as he watches them dance.

They return and sit down. I stare hard at the door, willing my dad to come through it. As the adults talk, my leg bounces under the table. I'm trapped.

A few minutes later, Don asks me again to dance. The floor is full of people twirling and smiling. My favorite type of dance is being played—1-2-3 cha cha, 1-2-3 cha cha.

"No, I don't want to dance." I hope he is hurting. He doesn't get to walk back in my life and pretend to be someone who cares about me. He hasn't been stuck on an island cut off from society. I slide my hands underneath my active legs. Why did he choose now to meet us?

The restaurant door opens. Sunshine wraps around Dad. My heart quiets. Within minutes, Dad and I are dancing a fox-trot. I tell Dad about Don wanting to dance with me and how I turned him down.

"Steph, you need to dance with him."

"Why?"

"Just dance with him. He's trying to get to know you and Brandon."

"It's a little late for that."

As we head back to the table, Dad says to Don, "Steph's ready to dance with you."

I want to kick Dad. I'd rather go see the dentist than dance with this absentee father.

The music changes and Don comes around the table and gives me his arm. I walk past him to the dance floor. I'm close enough to smell his smoky cologne. Dad wears the spicier Baron cologne. Don moves his body but shuffles his feet; it's clear he doesn't know how to ballroom dance. He pulls me closer to him. His hand is softer than Dad's, probably because he doesn't do any manual labor like my dad does sometimes. I can't wait to sit back down.

"My dad wins dancing contests," I yell over the music. "His students love him."

Don smiles. The music ends and we head back to the table. My heart hammers. I'm glad that's over.

Our food arrives. The smell of roast beef and gravy, mashed potatoes, and carrots fills my nose. Yeast rolls lie covered in the middle of the table. I avert my eyes from Don and talk only to my parents. Brandon soaks up every word Don says.

"Where do you live?" Brandon asks.

"We live in Sioux Falls, South Dakota," Don replies. "Joanna is from there."

"Do you and Joanna have children?"

"No. Joanna has a daughter, Michelle. I was married between your mom and Joanna. I have three children with that wife."

I slide up in my chair. Doesn't that mean I have three more siblings? I cut in. "What are their names and how old are they?" Maybe I can find a sister or brother I can be close to.

"The oldest one is Don, named after me. He's a year or so younger than you. Then I have another daughter named Staci and a younger son named Matt. Staci's ten and Matt is eight."

"Where do they live?"

"In Atlanta, with their mother."

I feel my heart race.

"So, we're related."

"They're your half siblings," Don says. "You share me as your birth father."

So much to think about. The others move on to talk about Sioux Falls as I slither back in my chair. I don't even try to picture where South Dakota is. I scan plates to see how soon we can leave. Still a lot of food to be eaten. I slide further down in my chair and take a deep breath. Sometimes my anger surprises me: I don't know I'm feeling angry until something sets me off. It's like a bomb sitting inside me. I scare myself sometimes when I can't make it stop.

Later, we make our way to our cars. A pressure lifts from my shoulders as I slip into the backseat. I'm finished with this meet-your-father gathering. Questions I wasn't aware of have been answered. He exists, he isn't handsome, and he's chosen not to meet us for thirteen years. And there are three more of us.

# CHAPTER 3

I'm seven years old. It's 1969. My hand flies up when my second-grade teacher, Miss Johnson, asks who would like to rub her shoulders today during story time.

"Okay Stephanie," Ms. Johnson says. "Come on up."

She picks my best friend, Carmen, as well.

My small hands knead Miss Johnson's right shoulder. My heart swells while classmates look at us. I feel my whole face smiling. Her fleshy arms give way under my fingers. Powder scents drift past my nose. Just when my hands begin to fatigue, a teenager walks in.

"Class, this is my seventeen-year-old son. He will join us for movie time."

*He's cute. I wonder how he got out of school.*

"Stephanie, you and Carmen get to walk with him to the auditorium too."

I got picked to rub her shoulders, and now I get to walk with her son to see the movie. *Wow! This is my lucky day!*

I smell the musty air as I hold hands with my teacher's son and walk the wide, wooden halls lined with cast-iron radiators. Carmen holds his other hand. Our footsteps are lost in the sounds of hundreds of others, as students flock to Missionary Ridge's auditorium. I swing my feet in the connected, hardwood folding seats, feeling the hard edge dig into the back of my leg under my skirt. I jump up and feel the imprints on my legs and walk around the small space between the seats. Carmen sits on his right side and I on his left.

Students file in and fill up the seats all around us. It seems that everyone is talking at once. Laughter, mixed with teachers' shouts to quiet down, fill the auditorium. I sit down. As the 8mm projector lights up the screen, the voices quiet down and I feel the teenager's hand find its way into my panties.

I hear Carmen tell him no.

*Why didn't I say no? It's too late. I missed the moment. It all happened so fast.*

Forget the movie. I only feel his hand rubbing me. He explores my private parts. I feel wet down there. Pleasure and guilt flow through me. *Someone help me. I don't know what to do. I wish I had said no. Does his mother know he does this? I don't like Miss Johnson anymore. I don't like him.*

Later, as I am driven home, all I want to do is take a bubble bath to clean myself. Thoughts swirl through my head. *Did I cause this to happen? Everyone will know what he did.* Shame and embarrassment keep my mouth shut. I add this secret to my heart space. A darkness settles over me.

School carries on as if nothing happened. I nod my head and pretend to do the same. Missionary Ridge Elementary and I become the keeper of secrets. I imagine this big, wooden building holds lots of secrets. My hands remain in my lap the next time Miss Johnson calls for volunteers. Gone are the impulses to be heard and seen. Maybe the quiet observer is the one who remains safe.

Later in the year, I stop Mr. Bailey, the principal, in the hall. He holds my face in his hands. His expression reminds me of my pediatrician's on visits. Their eyes hold both compassion and sorrow. I guess Mr. Bailey knows Brandon and I were abandoned by our birth father too.

I push these thoughts from my mind. I don't like thinking I was abandoned. Instead, I like thinking the man died.

"Mr. Bailey," I say, "some boy was trying to look up my dress when I was swinging today." Anger flushes my cheeks with righteous indignation.

He smiles and makes clucking sounds. "That's terrible," he says. "I'm sorry that happened to you."

Mr. Bailey gets me and feels the same way I do.

Days later, announcements are made in our auditorium. Mr. Bailey shares a story about a boy trying to look up a girl's dress while she swung on the blacktop. Laughter fills the high auditorium ceiling. I join in until a lightning bolt of recognition hits me. My hand covers my mouth as I tighten my eyes to keep tears from flowing. Shame and embarrassment flow through me again. This is my story he's telling. *How could he?* I add three more *do not trust* notes to my heart space for Miss Johnson, her son, and Mr. Bailey.

# CHAPTER 4

It's the beginning of April 2020. Mom and Dad celebrate their birthdays this month. I need to figure out what to get them. Years ago, we would have celebrated together.

I eat oatmeal and read my Bible. My finger lingers on Psalm 51:10-12: "Create in me a clean heart, O God, and renew a right spirit within me. Cast me not from your presence and take not your Holy Spirit from me . . ." I'm aware of how my heart melts when I read my favorite passage. I have turned to this psalm in times of struggle.

I pull leashes from a hook. The dogs and I step outside for our daily stroll. Contrails fill the mixed-blue sky while birds call to each other. The dogs keep their ears pointed up as they walk. My mind wanders to my childhood. I remember being eight years old, standing barefoot in a rocky pullover by our mailbox. My parents hadn't been married long. I looked up at our brick, split-level house and decided I would not wait hand and foot on my future husband the way my mom did. Like how a towel would appear on my parents' bed while Dad took a shower. If you blinked, you'd miss the sleight of hand where Mom replaced the towel with clothes as Dad dried himself.

I marvel at how young I was when I made this decision. Why did Mom feel compelled to wait on Dad? Why did he let her?

Pollen lies thick on the dark mailboxes. I sneeze and the pups jump. I laugh at them and at another memory. I'm sixteen and attending a parenting class at my church.

"Everyone, break into small groups," the leader says.

Chairs scrape while circles are formed. I sit amidst adults. I'm happy to be here. I want to learn about childrearing. This class seems like a good place to start.

"Stephanie." Rick, one of the group members, addresses me.

"Yes."

"Why are you here?"

"What do you mean?"

"Do you have a child in the closet or something?"

The other group members snicker. I laugh too.

"No, I don't have a child. But I want to learn about parenting."

I wanted to learn a different way of parenting. I knew I wanted to change some of the familial cycles I was growing up with. My grandmother married when she was fourteen and my mom when she was sixteen. Men meant more to my mom than she did to herself.

I knew I wouldn't set out clothes or towels or pack my future spouse's suitcase. He and I would share in all aspects of our marriage. With my life and my future children's lives in mind, I read everything I could, like *I'm Okay, You're Okay,* in my late teenage years. By the time I was nineteen, therapy was recommended for me. I'm so thankful it was.

Back at home with the dogs, I make a simple dinner and turn on the news as I wait for Mike to come home. Stores and businesses may shut down. The Italian people warn us that we have about two weeks before our country will look like theirs—hospitals overrun, staff shortages, and deaths. Oh, so many deaths. It's early April and I hear a prediction we may reach over two hundred thousand deaths before Covid-19 runs its course.

It's strange to cancel appointments. I don't know when I've missed having my teeth cleaned. Our house remains empty except for Mike and me. Friends' laughter and conversations and overnight guests are put on hold. I'm lucky I didn't catch Covid-19 last month when I played in a pickleball tournament before I knew about the virus.

Annie barks outside to let me know Mike is home. A few seconds later, he steps through the door.

"Hey, Steph," he says. "I'm going to dry my clothes and take a shower. I'll be right down."

"Okay."

I finish up our dinner and bring it to the den.

*Wheel of Fortune, Jeopardy,* and sports are regulars on our television screen. The news is a recent addition. Since I stay home, I no longer get this information through the radio in my car. I miss driving. I miss normal—like having lunch with my girlfriends every two weeks, playing pickleball with my friends, and going to church every Sunday. Now I feel safe in the abnormal.

Mike returns and sits six feet away. I can smell his washed body from this distance. We eat in front of the TV.

"How was your day?" he asks.

"Good. The pups and I took our usual walk. I thought about some of the decisions I made as I was growing up. Today I finished writing about my experience at Missionary Ridge and about meeting my birth father for the first time. I knew I wanted to change the way I did things when I became a parent."

"And you did."

"Yeah, I did. I'm grateful for the people God put in my life to guide me. Writing my memoir brings both pain and relief and seems to decrease my feelings of vulnerability."

His hazel eyes crinkle at the corners as he smiles behind his mask.

"I'm so glad you have the time to write now."

"Me too."

As the TV drones on, I think about the changes Mike has made for my sake. I have a deep need for physical contact, so we scrape our elbows together for touch and, like bears, we rub our backs together in our new form of a hug. Our roles have reversed. Now Mike goes to the stores and shops for our food and home supplies while I remain cocooned at home. Our house fills with my breath and Mike's masked breaths. I don't need to wear a mask since Mike is my only point of contact, but allergies prevent me from opening our windows to invite in nature and airflow.

"What is Colombia?" I smile at my sweet husband as he answers the questions on *Jeopardy.*

Cleaning our home is on me again. I know how to clean, because Mom was a clean freak. She had me washing the dishes before I was tall enough to reach the sink. If not for my dad's smoking, I believe our house would have smelled like lemon Pledge and Comet. I'm not happy to be doing this chore again, but I feel safer minimizing the amount of contact with other people.

I notice how technology is filling in gaps. Mike begins seeing patients through telemedicine. The new buzzword is *Zoom*. My girlfriends who are part of a group I started years before, called Good Vibes, want to learn how to use Zoom so we can continue to connect.

Change upsets me to the core. I feel dazed by it. So much so, I even eat the same foods for breakfast (oatmeal) and lunch (spinach sandwich with hummus), and I'll exhaust an author's entire body of work before trying a new genre. I fight change through gritted teeth. Even though I know that it's the only constant, it doesn't settle well with me.

I experienced a lot of change growing up, so I cling to the familiar like a tick on a dog. When I was twelve, my mom changed out my old threadbare, red velvet bedspread with a new one while I was at school. When I got home, I went ballistic.

"Where's my bedspread!" I yelled. "I want my old bedspread back on. I don't like this one. I don't need a new one."

My twelve-year-old hands yanked the new one off and I went in search of my old one. Tears threatened to spill, but I held them in check. I remember thinking that if I were to start crying I wouldn't be able to stop—like I'd fall in a pit and not be able to climb out.

"Stephanie Lee Salmon," Mom said with her hands on her hips. "I threw your old one in the trash. And that is that."

When *Jeopardy* is over, I take our plates to the kitchen and reach for the calendar. My finger runs along a week in the month of February. Monday: photo shoot for a business, pickleball; Tuesday: lunch with my women's group; Wednesday: pickleball, acupuncture, and lunch with a friend; Thursday: allergy/asthma doctor and dinner with one of our goddaughters; Friday: pickleball. All while taking care of our home, buying groceries and cooking, taking the pups out every three to four hours, and driving out of town for four of these events. I shake my head and return to the den.

Now the sound of our household footsteps slows down. The ringing of my cell phone slows down too. I give way from connecting with family and friends in person to seeing their faces on Zoom. Brooke joins the teletherapy community.

Google Duo allows us to meet, albeit with a pixelated version of ourselves.

I allow mail to pile up on our dining room table and ignore it for days. When Mike brings home groceries, the recycled bags look like centurions lined up on the floor next to the granite island. In his mask, he tosses oranges to me one at a time. All the groceries run through chlorine-soaked washcloths before finding their place in the refrigerator or pantry.

The rhythm of life changes every day. Church doors close. We watch Sunday services on our TV via social media. Worshiping at home feels strange. We fit ourselves into our church clothes and sit apart on our respective couches, our eyes glued to the TV. One dog sleeps beside me and the other beside Mike.

Our church family writes comments to each other, asking for specific prayers.

"I need prayers for my cousin," one person says. "He has Covid and is in the hospital." Another person says, "I miss being together. I hope this virus dies soon."

My faith is as embedded in me as breathing, but it has taken a hit during this pandemic. My fear of not being able to breathe has taken over. I think of Job and how he withstood so many flesh-tearing trials, and how my faith is being tested. Reading through my raggedy Bible every day and praying my prayers throughout the day are rituals I cling to during this threat.

At night, as I lie in bed, I say the Serenity Prayer: *God, grant me the serenity to accept the things I cannot change, the courage to change the things I can, and the wisdom to know the difference.* I add the Lord's Prayer, hoping for a faith cure. I thank God for all sorts of things, like my family, the pillow, a warm bed. My survival skills work overtime.

In regular times, the truth for me is found in faith. This faith forms my very being. This faith feels like a beating heart—constant and life-giving, guiding me away from self-centeredness and anger and toward gratefulness. I want to draw from this well every day but am coming up short.

Another Bible passage that resonates for me right now is Romans 8:26-27: "In the same way, the Spirit helps us in our weakness. We do not know what we need to pray for, but the Spirit himself intercedes for us through wordless groans." I know I am being carried right now. I am confident of this assistance.

Most mornings, when I wake up, my pulse quickens in its semiconscious state. *I need to stay safe. Wait. Remember all that you are grateful for.* Like a ping-pong game, fear and faith battle it out—much like my thoughts about the past and how I reach for the present. This game of past-and-present needs to end. The back-and-forth leaves me exhausted and off-balance.

I yawn. "Hey, babe," I say. "I'm heading to bed. My brain is buzzing with thoughts, but my body has other ideas."

"I love you. Sleep well, Steph."

"I love you too. Nighty night."

I crawl into bed and pray out of a heart full of thankfulness, fear, and need for direction. The sounds of Mike cleaning the kitchen fall away. I roll to my side and think about the time when I felt the weight of God's hand on me. I fall asleep reminiscing about hearing His voice.

# CHAPTER 5

It's 1971 and I'm nine. My friend Amy moves to the country on the other side of Chattanooga. She leaves behind a huge hole. For the past year and a half, Amy and I played together every day after we got home from our different schools. She lived across the street from me in one side of a duplex. Sometimes she came to church with us. In the summertime, she would come with me and my family to the lake. We camped with my dad's brothers and families. Dad would throw us kids in the water, launching us as far as he could.

"One more time, Mr. Davis," Amy says. "Please."

"Me next," I yell.

Amy's stepfather, Michael, is a live wrestler. Sometimes I'd go with Amy and her mom to watch him compete. The first time I went with them, my parents told me I was in for a different type of entertainment, that it wouldn't be the same as my brother Brandon's matches.

"Steph," Dad says. "This is not the same type of wrestling you're used to. This is make-believe. They don't get hurt, but they act like it. You'll see."

I meet Amy's family across the street. Mr. Jones is already at Memorial Auditorium getting ready. When we walk in, the auditorium is loud and full of cigarette smoke. In the middle, I see a ring with ropes like a boxing ring. My eyes widen.

"Mrs. Jones," I ask, "are those midgets?"

My eyes follow these short, thick-bodied women as they climb up the wrestling ring and flip themselves through the ropes. The women throw each other around and don't listen to the referee. They remind me of clowns at a circus.

Mrs. Jones leans over and yells into my ear. The noise of people laughing and clapping makes it hard for me to hear her. "Yes, Steph. Those are midgets."

I've never seen anything like this. Live wrestling is wild.

At our homes, Amy and I spend hours playing and sharing secrets. Sometimes I'd wear Mr. Jones's wrestling boots to play in. When Amy comes to my fast-pitch softball games, her blonde hair and goofy smile are easy to spot. We are inseparable. Until she moves away.

Mom knows how devastated I am since Amy left. A few months after the move, Mom drives me to her house for a weekend sleepover.

We ride her stepdad's riding lawnmower and play on her unicycle—we get a lot of bruises. She teaches me how to play Rook.

For me, Sundays are church days. Amy and her parents do not attend church, but I had noticed a small white Baptist church down the road from her house when Mom dropped me off. So on Sunday I talk Amy into coming with me. Her mother gives her permission for us to go alone. "Come straight home after the service," she says.

The church sits around a bend and out of sight. Ten-year-old Amy and nine-year-old me wear dresses and walk a quarter of a mile to the church. The door seems to open of its own accord. Adults stand and talk in a low-ceilinged room. Some sit at long tables. No pews, no altar.

Amy looks up at the adults and back at me. "Steph, I'm going home. I don't know these people."

I turn to her and nod my head, but I am not quite ready to abandon my plan to be in church, even though I wish she would stay with me. I don't know these people either. I take a deep breath and stay rooted where I am.

Her simple white dress disappears behind the door. I am lost in a sea of adults, and I realize that the service is over. I wish I had known their schedule. Does it count that I came to church but missed the service? I want to cry, but I don't know anyone here and I don't feel safe. I wanted to experience a church service, with taking communion and singing hymns—not talking with people I don't know.

Someone asks me who I am. I want to say, *A Christian trying to go to church who didn't think to check what time your service started.* I shrug my shoulders and scan the room and see that there is nothing for me here.

I feel alone; in fact, I am alone. I feel separated from God. Maybe I need to think of God every day and not just on Sundays.

My shoulders droop as I walk back to Amy's. I look down and see the gravel and cracks that form the old road. *I feel like I let God down.* Kneeling on the rocky asphalt, I ask Him to forgive me.

"God, I'm so sorry I missed church today. I didn't mean to. I'm really, really sorry. I didn't mean to disappoint You." I wipe tears from my face.

If I were at home, I would have been at church with my church family. Being at church feels as important to me as being at school. Sometimes my parents drop Brandon and me off for Sunday school while they go eat breakfast together.

Mom always shows back up for church, sometimes with Dad and sometimes not.

Still kneeling on the road, I feel a light pressure on my shoulder, like a hand, coupled with a sense of safety and love. It's as if God is telling me that He is always with me and that He loves me. I have heard this assurance at church, but now I am hearing it from GOD himself.

Brushing my knees off, I stand and feel an incredible sense of belonging and forgiveness. In that moment, I realize He loves me whether I go to church or not. He loves me no matter what I do or do not do. God loves me *all the time.*

My tears dry up and my face stretches with a wide smile. I hold this memory close to me like a security blanket. I won't ever let go.

I realize guilt has become a close companion. I replay over and over the scene when the teenager put his hands in my panties. Having secrets isolates me from my mom and others, but I am too ashamed to share what happened to me. Guilt from not saying no to Miss Johnson's son stays with me. Even with this experience now with God, I find myself feeling like people might not love me if they knew. *If I don't fly right, I could be discarded like a piece of trash, just like my birth father discarded me.* As soon as I recognize that I'm drifting away from this God moment, I pull myself back in. God loves me and is with me. I tell myself, *hold on to that feeling of love, Steph.*

## CHAPTER 6

Mom and Dad ask Brandon and me to come into the den. It's September 1971 and I am about to start fourth grade.

"Brandon, Stephanie," Dad says. "Your mother and I have decided to move you to a different school."

"Why?" we ask in unison.

"It's a private school and we think you'll get a better education."

"I don't want to go to another school," says Brandon.

"Some of your friends from Missionary Ridge will be at your new school."

I stay quiet. I don't like change, but I'm not happy with Missionary Ridge after what Miss Johnson's son and Mr. Bailey did to me.

"The school is St. Stephen's Country Day School," Dad continues. "It's a Catholic school. The classroom sizes are small."

"I still don't understand why we need to move," Brandon says.

"Well, son, your mom and I think it's a better school. And there's a thing called desegregation happening in the public school system this year and we think it's a good time to switch."

"What's desegregation mean?" I ask.

"It means that more and more Black students will be bused to Missionary Ridge and other public schools. The school system wants to even out the schools between Black and White children."

"So?" I ask. "We already have Black friends. That's no big deal. They're no different from us." I always defend Black people when I hear slurs against them.

"I know, Stephanie," Mom pipes in. "But your dad and I think St. Stephen's will give you a better education than Missionary Ridge."

I feel myself heat up. I don't like that my parents think Black people would be bad for us at school. They are our friends. One of the teachers at Missionary Ridge is Black. I don't understand the problem.

"Why would you make us move because of Black people?" I ask.

"Stephanie, it isn't just that," Dad protests. "But case closed. You guys will start at St. Stephen's tomorrow. They are already in session, but you won't be far behind."

Brandon and I look at each other. This switch is out of the blue.

"Brandon," Mom says, "we need to buy some white shirts and clip-on ties for you. Steph, you'll be wearing uniforms with white shirts. I've already ordered them. They'll come in this week."

I'm confused by my parents' decision. I know some of my dad's relatives are prejudiced, but I didn't think my parents were. They say they aren't prejudiced, but if they are moving us to a private school because of busing . . . I think there's more to our being moved than the small class sizes. I think there's fear for them, or maybe just for Dad—being with Black people will be bad for us somehow. I don't get it.

The next day, I enter the fourth-grade classroom at this small school, which is much newer and brighter than Missionary Ridge. I'm late because of spending time with Sister Kathleen Marie, the principal, who explained the school rules. An empty desk sits in the middle of the room and I slide into it. The boy next to me leans over.

"Hey," he whispers. "I'm Tony."

"Hi. I'm Stephanie."

I smile. Tony smiles back. I can't wait to tell my parents that my first friend at the new school is Black.

The next morning, we gather in the school's nave downstairs.

"Please get out the music books in your pews," Father Schilling says.

I reach in the pew and pull out a worn music book. My head snaps up when I hear the priest belt out "Hey Jude." I love this song. When I didn't think things could get better, we sing "Let it Be." Turns out, our churches are similar. At the end, the priest blesses us. I look around and see my classmates using one hand to make the sign of the cross. That's different. Our steps sound flat against the rubber-tiled stairs as we make our way to our classrooms.

I think I'm going to like it here. The small class size and spread-out desks will force me to learn. I realize I should already know my multiplication tables. At Missionary Ridge, I was placed in mixed-level grades where we had over thirty students. In math, I used to look over a smart boy's shoulders to cheat. Those days are over. I hum "Hey Jude" in my head as I listen to my teacher. I see the colors from the stained glass windows downstairs. I smile. I like it here.

# CHAPTER 7

The aroma of sauteed fish and roasted broccoli float from the kitchen to the love seat where I sit. I watch the news, surrounded by our small dogs. It's mid-April 2020. Neither Mike nor I have the virus.

"Here, babe," Mike says as he hands me my plate of food.

"Dinner smells so good. Thank you for cooking. And thank you for your sweet note this morning. I love starting my day by reading one of your notes." Today's note was *I love you and am so glad you're my wife.*

He smiles. Our kitchen cabinets are filled with multicolored Post-it notes that Mike leaves me every morning.

"I love you, babe," I say.

"I love you more."

"Uh uh."

"Yes, I do."

I smile. We always say these words, but usually they are packed with action. When we don't need to isolate, we hold each other's hands and sit knee to knee.

"Do you remember what people at St. Matthias' said when we moved here?" I ask.

"That our kissing and hugging and holding hands would fade."

"Yep, but we still do these things. I'm the luckiest girl in the world."

Mike sits on the couch catty-corner to me. I'm cross-legged on the love seat with the dogs next to me. I use a pillow as a table for my dinner plate. We lower our heads as Mike says the blessing.

As he finishes, I am also grateful for the meal delivery service we've been using for the last several years.

Given the virus, more people are turning to similar options, and I recommend our food service to others. We eat better than we ever have. Fresh, organic meals are delivered to our front door, just needing us to cook them—anything to reduce time at the grocery store.

As we watch TV, seeing people hugging and talking close to each other in commercials makes me cringe. My survival instincts are on high alert. I remind myself they were filmed before the virus. I relax again.

After we eat, I collect our plates and return to the kitchen. I take a deep breath and inhale the full range of smells floating in the air and smile. I look around at the dirty dishes on the granite countertops and in our sinks. I feel grateful for this mess. We have delicious food to eat and a convenient way to clean it up. Not everyone does. I run warm water over the plates and stack them in the dishwasher.

In terms of job security, I'm also thankful Mike is a healthcare worker. Since my early retirement from nursing, I home-educated our sons. Later I returned to school for photography. Now I'm a freelance photographer and drone pilot and can adjust my schedule. Not everyone is so fortunate.

Protected from the virus at home, I have also gained time to write during the pandemic.

As a young girl, I received gifts of pink diaries on various occasions. Each one had a small lock to keep the inside private. The locks never worked well, so I wrote very little.

I turned to writing journals after I took an elective class in high school called Spiritual Journey. One of the priests at my Catholic high school instructed the class. Father Al taught us how keeping a journal benefits our spiritual well-being. In the beginning, I wrote as if someone else might read it. I kept everything on the surface or wrote what sounded best.

For one of my first journals, while doing missionary work in Costa Rica in 1981, I typed up the handwritten journal. Near the end of it, I critiqued the content. "This logbook (i.e. journal) portrays many different characteristics of its writer. Sometimes I wish I had written on more of an emotional level—including the times when *feeling* experiences occurred—rather than on factual data."

Over the years, I learned to write with abandon, as I'm doing now with my memoir. When I met my husband, I had already filled thirty-two notebooks with journal entries.

My fingers type while my heart unloads my past. Like a grocery list, I want to get it all down so my brain can let go of these memories. In the mornings, my chest feels heavy. My dreams are vivid and complex. Someone's trying to kill me or lead me away from comfort. I lie still running through my dreams and stare at my cathedral ceiling. It's as if I've run a marathon. My heart races. I feel pinned to my bed like a mummy. I want to wake up in the mornings feeling fresh and ready for the day.

When I return from the kitchen, *Jeopardy* is on. "Man, Alex Trebek is amazing," I say. "He's facing his stage IV pancreatic cancer with grit and determination. Wouldn't it be something if he somehow beat it?"

"Yes, it would."

I send up a prayer for Alex. *Please give him the strength to fight this disease.*

I lean back in the love seat and glance at my sweet husband. He is dedicated to protecting me by wearing a mask when he is on the main floor with me. He has a collection of pediatric-oriented masks that nursing staff make for him.

Later, I get up and stretch.

"I'm heading to bed."

Mike gets up too. We rub our backs together. Our heads caress each other, meshing hair to hair. My chest rises and falls as I close my eyes. I long to wrap my arms around him and feel his lips on mine.

He grabs the pups and takes them upstairs. "I love you, Steph."

"I love you too. Sleep well."

I feel lonely. The words *patience* and *intention* snap to focus in my mind. But I still feel vulnerable. During the day, Brooke comforts me by keeping my focus on the things I can change, and weekly Zoom meetings with my girlfriends help me feel less alone in my fears. But nighttime is a different story.

In bed, I recall the day our priest, Jim Curtis, suggested that I needed therapy. I was nineteen years old.

"Dr. Curtis," I say. "May I talk to you after the church service?"

"Yes, just give me a few minutes."

As I wait in his office, I hear his shoes tapping against the floor. He walks in and closes the doors.

"What's going on, Steph?"

"I just want you to know, if we get a computer and the screen gets busted, you'll know who did it."

He takes a deep breath and looks at me as if he can see all of me.

"Steph, your feelings towards our getting a computer are not about the computer. I recommend counseling."

My jaw drops. What does he mean? I respect him so much and love being a part of the governing body at our church, but I don't want a computer here. They're dehumanizing. They'll take over our world, just like I read in *1984*. I feel tears inside me. I can't keep the computers out of my world. Why does that mean I need counseling?

"I have someone in mind for you. She works for the Department of Family and Children Services."

"I can't afford counseling."

"You can afford her. She charges based on your income."

As I lie in bed now, I realize I haven't thought about this conversation in a long time.

I slide further under my cool sheets and close my eyes in my queen-size bed, only to toss and turn. People are dying. I don't want to go there, but I can't help it. My fear of dying from Mike's exposure has lessened, but it's the unknown that keeps me from sound sleep.

I long to feel my husband's strong arms around me. I wish my hugging pillow was Mike. Instead, I thrash around the bed and repeat the Serenity and Lord's Prayers. My thoughts hover above the present before landing on past times of vulnerability. These memories plague me; they always have. I roll to my right side, close my eyes, and try to settle into sleep.

# CHAPTER 8

"Stephanie, do we need to take you to the hospital?" Mom asks.

It is 1974 and I'm twelve. She and Dad are crowding my small bedroom, sitting on kitchen chairs beside my bed. Coughing shakes my body and my bed. I can't seem to stop coughing. It's hard to breathe. *I don't want to scare them.*

"No, I'm okay."

Dad's eyes are pinned on me. His mouth forms a straight line. The humidifier spits out water and makes a loud buzzing sound. Mom lifts my head to give me more of her concoction of honey and whiskey. She steadies the coffee cup and spoons some onto my tongue. Part of me wonders how good this spiked honey is for me, but since it makes Mom feel better, I sip it down. I've lost count of how many spoonfuls I've had. Vicks VapoRub burns my eyes from where Mom has slathered it on my chest. I cough up more junk and feel the pain worsening in my ribs.

I think back to the weekend before when our church youth group spent two days at an old hunting lodge. Our bikes and duffle bags were tossed into a large truck lined with coarse, dusty hay at church. We climbed into the back behind our stuff and rode all the way to the lodge. I had spent extra time in the hay truck long after it was parked while my ex-boyfriend, Jimmy, and I made out.

I loved being with my friends and had so much fun. I wish I were back there now. My coughing seemed to start after I got home and hasn't stopped. I can't catch my breath. I suck in air like a fish out of water, gasping for breath.

Mom and Dad stay beside me all night, asking me if I need to go to the hospital. I feel my body tiring. How many more breaths do I have? I'm light-headed and sweaty. I want to stop coughing and go to sleep. I'm hot and sticky.

I guess I finally went to sleep, but I am very sick because now Dad is carrying me to our station wagon. I feel safe in his arms. I notice the sun has come up and then I fall asleep again. I'm awakened as I'm brought into a building. A lot of noise and activity surround me. I want my dad with me. Mom tells me he is parking the car. I feel a prick in my arm. I am being held up for a chest X-ray. I just want to sleep. Before I know it, I throw up everywhere, including on the nurse's feet. I taste the honey and alcohol in my mouth, plus the vomit. Yuck. She gives me another shot in my arm.

*Where am I?* I come in and out of sleep, aware that nurses are pouring something behind my head. A plastic tent surrounds my body. Cool air flows around me. My long brown hair is wet and sticking to me. I try to lift my head to see where my parents are. They're hunched together on a couch on the left side of my bed. I'm not afraid anymore and I drift back to sleep.

I open my eyes sometime later. Mom and Dad stand beside me, looking down at me through the foggy plastic.

"What's wrong with me?"

"Honey, you have double pneumonia," Mom answers. "Both of your lungs are filled with pneumonia. Are you cold?"

"Not really. Why am I in this tent?"

"They're keeping oxygen in there to help you breathe," explains Dad. "You really scared us."

"I didn't mean to. I thought I had bronchitis again."

"No, hon," Dad says, "you're sicker than that."

My stomach growls and my parents fall all over themselves to get me something to eat. I must have slept through some meals. A nurse comes in to check on me.

"Look who's awake," she says. "We've been worried about you. How are you feeling?"

"Hungry!"

As I eat the hamburger steak, macaroni and cheese, and Jell-O, my parents tell me about the past several days. In the absence of an intensive care unit, nurses have stayed beside me around the clock since my arrival. I swallow more than food as I listen. I take in all that my parents tell me. *It sounds like I was close to dying. I hope I get better soon.*

Over the days, I amuse myself with word-search magazines called *Seek-A-Word*. I like looking at the flowers that line my window and side table. I read cards as soon as they come. Visitors come and go. I'm not allowed to bring the remote control for my bed and TV into my tent. I can't see the television very well anyway through the plastic and misty air.

My mind drifts to my outdoors life. I'm playing basketball and softball and am the neighborhood football quarterback. I'm also the catcher for my fast-pitch softball team. I've been catching since I was nine years old. After I begged to catch, my opportunity came when our regular catcher was sick. The first time behind the plate was pure hell. I got whacked over and over again by the ball and the hitter's bat. I fell into the umpire many times, as if I were a bumper car. At first I hated catching, but my stubbornness and pride kept me behind the plate; I told my coach that I loved it. When our regular catcher moved up the next year, I took over. Once I figured out how to stop the ball, avoid the bat, and keep my balance, I became quite good. I feel special wearing my chest protector, shin guards, and mask. I love the dirt. Playing sports gives me confidence.

I hear my hospital door open. I see my current fast-pitch coaches, Barney and C.E., enter. I smile. Both have mustaches, but Barney has brown hair and C.E. has bushy black hair. They sit on the couch by the window and look forlorn. *I must look bad.* Soon, Barney makes jokes and has Mom and me laughing. I begin to cough my deep, congested cough and then Barney gets quiet.

"I'm okay," I reassure him. "It feels good to get this stuff up."

"Yogi, I didn't mean to make you cough so much," Barney replies.

"No. It's good for me."

We joke some more before they leave. I love hearing my nickname. An earlier coach of mine christened me Yogi after Yogi Berra, the famous New York Yankees catcher. I'm fearless when it comes to throwing runners out. Even though I'm skinny, my right arm has superpowers that catch teams off guard.

The priests at my Episcopal church visit me almost every day at the hospital. They wear black priest shirts with a white collar and church pants. I feel loved because of all the attention I'm getting. My doctor and his partners come see me every day too. I know they have to visit, so I am not as excited when they come by. After I have been living inside my tent home for two weeks, my pediatrician stops by. His thick glasses make his eyes look huge.

"Stephanie, we've been weaning you off your oxygen, and your chest X-ray looks good, so you get to go home today."

I'm excited to go. I miss school and my friends and my bed. Two weeks is a long time to miss school, plus the few days I was sick at home. Mom and Dad load up my hospital stuff, flowers, and cards. I follow them outside to our blue, wood-paneled station wagon and discover the air is hard to breathe in. I stop in the parking lot to catch my breath. *Oh, no. Am I hooked on oxygen? I want my oxygen back.* After a few seconds, I'm able to breathe and climb into the car. I keep my worry to myself. By the time Dad pulls into our driveway, my lungs have adjusted to regular air again.

Days go by and life gets back to normal. At least that is what I think until Mom takes me to a follow-up appointment with my pediatrician.

# CHAPTER 9

Mom and I walk into the pediatric group's office. I look around at the linoleum flooring, drab colors, and a crib in the corner, and want to turn around and leave. Bronchitis has brought me here a number of times, but today, I'm not in the mood. My body is betraying me and taking me places I don't want to go. I look around with angry eyes. I don't want to be here. I'm tired of being around doctor stuff. I want to be left alone. Mom attempts a game of *I Spy*, but I shake my head. I want to brood.

After forever, a nurse steps into the waiting room and calls my name. I linger behind Mom and don't look the nurse in the eye as I walk past her. We are directed to the first room behind the waiting room door. The room is small with beige-colored walls, two chairs, and an examination table.

Dr. Corey explains that I will have an allergy test done. I must wear yet another hospital gown. Mom watches me slip off my top and ties my gown. Wearing a gown puts me back at the hospital where my identity was stripped down to a bracelet. I lie face down on the table for the test. I don't have any say in this. I want it to be over; I don't like being here.

The nurse enters with a tray and something that looks like a thimble. She makes a grid of rows on my back with sticks. They both tickle and sting me. When she finishes, she cleans up and leaves. I glare at my mother as if it's her fault. Within a few minutes, my back feels on fire. I'm itching like crazy.

"Mama, scratch my back!" My heart rate increases.

"Honey, I can't."

"*Please!*" My eyes now plead with her, and she sees me panic. Both of us are in tears.

"Get the doctor, I can't take this!"

Mom leaves the room while I do my best to remain on my stomach. The itching is getting worse. My toughness evaporates with each passing second.

Mom returns with Dr. Corey, who takes one look at my back and leaves again.

"Where'd he go?"

The doctor returns quickly with more people wearing lab coats.

"Please get this off my back! I can't take the itching anymore."

A sound escapes from Dr. Corey before he explains the results of my test to the others.

"Stephanie's test started a few minutes ago and her body is already overreacting to the serum."

A nurse enters and begins to wipe off the extracts.

Dr. Corey continues. "Stephanie just spent a few weeks in the hospital recovering from double pneumonia. Now we know why."

The other people shuffle out of the tiny room, leaving just Dr. Corey with my mother and me. I sit up and reach my hand back and feel lots of warm bumps. I'm ready to get out of there. I don't want to hear what he has to say. Mom stands up and rubs my back and ties my gown and my heart rate slows down. I know I didn't pass this test, but I want my life to go back to normal.

"Steph," Dr. Corey says, "you are allergic to lots of things out in the world. They triggered an asthma attack that led to your pneumonia."

"I have asthma now?"

"Yes, you do. The nurse will come back in and explain to you and your mom what you need to stay away from and the changes you need to make so you don't get sick like that again."

I look over at Mom, whose eyes have filled with tears. I dress and wrap my arms around myself for comfort. I don't like feeling so vulnerable.

A nurse knocks and joins Mom and me in this hellhole of a room. The three of us look at a sheet of paper she brought that shows all the allergens I reacted to—all thirty-three of them. There are plus signs with numbers beside the allergens my body hyper-responded to. This paper holds such precious information about me, and yet it isn't even neatly typed up. Once again, I feel like a discarded piece of trash. The nurse further explains the numbers by saying the higher the number—four being the highest—the more I am allergic. My results were mostly fours with a few threes and twos thrown in.

Then began a litany of *don'ts.* "You will need to get rid of any feather pillows, carpet, and stuffed animals. Clothes should be the only thing in your closet. And Stephanie, you are allergic to most grasses and trees in this area as well, so you'll need to be careful when you go outside."

After that, I break from the trio. I feel like a punching bag every time the nurse ticks off another thing I can't do or be around. My life is over. If I were a comic book character, steam would be coming out of my ears. *STOP!* I quit listening to the nurse. At least I'm not allergic to the far-out green and orange beads that hang between our foyer and small den. Incense wasn't mentioned either. But I *am* a freak who needs to live in a vacuum or risk getting pneumonia again.

I don't remember leaving that miserable place. Mom takes me across the street to the Baskin-Robbins ice cream parlor. We sit by a window. I'm sporting a white, flat cap with an auto logo on it, as if I'm Italian. I wear a leather bracelet and bell-bottoms. Being cool is important to me; I carry my coolness everywhere I go, as a badge of honor. Before taking off my cap and dropping my head on the table, I give Mom an earful of my wrath. The last drops of enthusiasm for life seep out of me and down to the sticky floor.

Rolling in grass, hiking, and being around cats, dogs, and other animals could send me right back to the emergency room. I love the outdoors and now I am allergic to it. The ice cream loses its flavor as I think about how much my life will change. Mom does her best to cheer me up, but my ears are too stopped up by anger to hear her. I want to blame someone or something. I want off this train of illness. But when my own body fights itself, there is no place to get off.

Mom gives me another night with my feather pillows. My new psychedelic carpet is up for further discussion. I love that long, red, orange, yellow, and black carpet. That night, I pull out feathers from the pillows and rub them in my face. *Take that, Dr. Corey.* Of course, on some level, I know he is not responsible for my allergies. I hug my pink stuffed hippopotamus harder as I cry myself to sleep.

A few months later, Mom comes into my room.

"Steph," she says, "Dr. Corey's office called. He wants to start you on weekly allergy shots to try and make you better."

"What? I'm not finished with all this?"

"No, honey. But just think, the shots may help you get over your allergies. There's an allergist who's just moved to town, a Dr. Kaplan. We have an appointment to see him this afternoon."

I flop on my bed. I feel punished somehow. When will I be like my friends? At recess, I stay inside and watch my friends play. Johnny's kicking off his shoe on the swings. I love that game. I want to be playing kickball on the hardtop too. I want to play. It's not fair! I hate allergies and asthma. I slump against the wall of the classroom, wanting to disappear. I feel the bottle of Benadryl in my pocket. I grab four pills and head to the water fountain, but swallow only two of them. *I can't even do this right.*

# CHAPTER 10

Coronavirus brings me back to that time of vulnerability. I did not escape allergies and asthma. They have clung to me like superglue on paper these past forty-seven years. Rolling in the grass and playing in the hay ended when I was twelve.

It's Sunday afternoon in late April 2020, and I'm organizing my medication for the week. Our backyard trees sway in the shadowy light. A Carolina wren chirps from the red oak tree outside my bathroom window. This tree is a favorite meeting spot for many different birds and squirrels.

I place the pills in their proper day or night compartment—green for morning and blue for evening. The medicines have increased as I've aged. I take four puffs a day from my inhalant to help prevent an asthma attack. A rescue inhalant always stays with me. Three other medications work to keep my allergies at bay.

As I snap each plastic lid closed, I think about all the years my arms were stuck with needle after needle and the time spent in allergists' offices. Immunotherapy never worked for me. After thirty years of off-and-on injections, my body was as reactive as it had been when I was twelve. These medications help reduce my symptoms, but unless a modern miracle occurs, I will have allergies and asthma until I die. Right now, I pray for a vaccine for Covid-19.

"Hey, Steph," Mike says. "Are you about ready to take a walk?"

"I'll be right there."

Mike and I leash our dogs and head outside. Leaves fill out while flowers burst through the ground and hummingbirds drink from feeders. They arrived early this spring. As we walk, I tell Mike about one of the dreams I had the night after the governor of our state decided to open Georgia just as the virus was picking up speed. I'm a vivid dreamer, and Mike is a great listener.

"My dream started off with me suddenly at a beach where there's a bar in the ocean and I'm thinking, oh, I have my camera with me. I'm thinking I'll take a picture of all these people who suddenly show up. They're in bathing suits, wearing sunglasses, slathered with suntan lotion, and drinking beer. I'm on a sidewalk and want to step off to get this documentary image of all these crowding people. And then I realize that I'm in the midst of them and I don't have a mask on. Nobody is wearing a mask. I decide to get out of there as fast as I can and turn to go back down the sidewalk. People are bumping into me and rubbing elbows with me. I throw my hands in front of my face to try to block the germs. I know that I've gotten the virus. There's no way I escaped it while being in that crowded group of people and in such close proximity. I was disgusted with myself and panicked. I ran as fast as I could."

Mike nods sympathetically.

"Obviously I'm worried about being exposed, but I also need a break from all the running around I do. I think I traveled about 310 miles per week before Covid. Just playing pickleball three times a week meant I traveled 150 miles. And I squeezed in time for groceries, time with friends, running our house, and my photography business. I'm tired just thinking about all the things I managed."

Our dogs walk beside us, listening to our voices and stopping briefly to relieve themselves. The scent of a sweet olive tree fills my nostrils well before we pass it. I take a deep breath and inhale the fresh fragrance of vanilla. I want to roll in it. On second thought, I might be allergic. I'll enjoy the smell from a distance.

"When we build our lake house, I want to plant several of these olive trees," I say.

"We will," Mike agrees.

"I wonder if there'll ever be a day when I wake up feeling refreshed and free from all the things that hold me down. My dreams are so thick and charged. They have been for most of my life. I cheat myself by the way I wake up and remain vigilant."

"I wish I could make it all go away for you. You're doing all you can do, Steph."

We look in each other's eyes until Mike is distracted by the song of a pileated woodpecker.

I smile as I watch my husband walk a short distance away. His eyes scan the trees for birds. He loves to photograph birds. I do too, but my arms and neck bother me too much right now to wield my long lens for this type of photography. Fibromyalgia also reminds me of my limits.

I want to hug him so badly. At least we have the pups to love on. It's not the same, but it's something.

Touch is my love language, and the absence of it leaves me aching. I miss Mike sitting next to me on the love seat, holding hands with our legs wrapped around each other. When this virus began and we knew we had to stay safe, our motto became "We are in this for the long haul." And we are.

# CHAPTER 11

"What's this?" I ask myself.

It's December of 1974 and I'm twelve years old. I recovered from double pneumonia just a few months before, but I'm getting to play at recess now. My parents caved when they saw how miserable I was.

I have just felt a lump. I look into the tiny bathroom mirror and notice a bump beside my left nipple. I'm flat- chested, so it's easy to see. What now? I need a break from body problems. A loneliness seeps in and wipes away any confidence I once had.

I'm not telling anyone about this lump, I decide. I do not want to go back to the hospital. I close my eyes to the mirror.

Toweling off each day from my shower and looking in the mirror becomes the new norm. Tension fills me every time I check myself. I want the mirror to be magical and remove this unwelcome growth. Running a hand over myself, I know the lump is getting bigger. The fast-growing changes scare me. Maybe it will go away. I make a wish, "Please leave my body," and pretend to blow out a candle.

A few months later, some male classmates stay the night at their friend Ronnie's house a few doors down from where several of us girls are spending the night. It is now March of 1975 and I'm thirteen years old. After we sneak outside, the boys come from the fringes of darkness and join us. Stephen, my boyfriend, climbs into my warm sleeping bag.

I need to share my secret. As the swelling grows, so does my anxiety.

"Feel this," I tell Stephen. I trust him.

He reaches under the sleeping bag and feels over my shirt. "Steph, you need to tell your parents."

My stomach churns. Telling them means bad things. I know this.

The next week, I find my mom. "Mom, I have a lump on my chest. I've had it for a few weeks, and it keeps getting bigger."

Mom's face distorts into a frown as she feels the hardness under my skin. She looks at me with fear-filled eyes. What I want to hear from her is that this lump is nothing to worry about. Instead, she jumps up and grabs the phone. I curl up on my bed and hug my stuffed hippo while I await my fate.

Once again, the pediatrician's office comes into view. We are escorted straight back into a small examination room. After the doctor feels the lump, he instructs Mom to take me to her gynecologist's office. Someone's always wanting to check me. The safe space of my room at home is long gone, since I can't hide from my body.

Mom drives us to Dr. Demos's office downtown. He is my grandmother's gynecologist and considered one of the best in Chattanooga. I couldn't care less. I clench my jaw the few minutes we sit in the stark waiting room. As the nurse calls for me, I realize I am bypassing adults who were here before me.

I feel cold and shaky as another doctor feels the lump. Without really looking at me, he instructs the nurse to move me into another examination room. I've become invisible except for my problem. I feel small, tossed around like a football.

"Take off your underwear and wrap this cover around you," the nurse tells me.

*What? No way.*

Mom cries, so I do as I am told.

*Help me,* my eyes plead. The table has the typical white paper sheet covering it but differs from the usual tables I've been on lately. This one has hard, cold stirrups for my feet. When Dr. Demos returns, he tells me that he will be examining me down below.

Some discussion floats in the air about finding a small enough instrument for me. Mom curls behind my left shoulder and cries in my ear as the doctor pushes his fingers into my vagina.

*Leave me alone,* I want to shout. *Stop.*

Did he tell me about this part? I grip the sides of the table. Darkness fills my vision as I close my eyes and clench my jaw. I grow angrier and angrier. Another nail is hammered into the casket of distrust I feel toward adults.

Memories of when I was seven years old flood past my darkened vision. Shame winds its way around my heart again. As in that experience with my teacher's son, my voice remains silent. Quiet suffering has become the new norm for me. I add this violation to my heart space.

Why did the doctor do this to me? The lump is near my breast, for God's sake.

Dr. Demos finishes by adding more goo to me and then puts a cold, hard instrument inside me. Fury fills me. I hate this man. Humiliation seeps through every limb on my body. Having my mom be a silent observer feels cruel; her power is lost in this room. Coldness grips as shaking overcomes my body. A blanket is wrapped around me before I dress.

*I should have kept my mouth shut. I wish I had not told Mom about this lump.*

The belief that life is hard and full of suffering seeps into my bones.

*My body is causing me harm. No one sees me, just my problem. I hate being touched by this old man. I don't care that he's a doctor.*

For the third time today, Mom drives me to another doctor's office. This one is for a surgeon named Dr. Graves. Here, I'm not taken right back to see him. The dark-paneled waiting room is full of adults wearing various bandages. Their eyes lift from their magazines to meet mine. Somehow, they seem to know I'm the patient and are curious about me. I want to tell them I don't know how I ended up here either, that today has been one of the worst days of my life.

When I make it to his examination room, Dr. Graves treats me like a person.

"You've had quite a day as I understand it," he says. His eyes smile at me.

I raise my hooded eyes to him. Is he really speaking to me? I relax my tired body a little. My hands open, while my heart rate slows. His voice is soothing as he asks me if I would mind sitting on the table for him.

"I'll be back in a few minutes while the nurse gets you ready," he says.

When my shirt is off and the paper top on, Dr. Graves returns. His large hands are warm and gentle. He feels around and tries moving the lump. He makes some encouraging remarks about how the tumor moves and appears to be intact. His gloves pop as he takes them off. The sound echoes in the uncarpeted room. His blue eyes smile at me again as he invites Mom and me to his office after I get dressed.

"We are going to need to take it out," Dr. Graves says. "The sooner the better. I don't think it will be anything, but we need to make sure. You're young to have a breast tumor."

I'm admitted to an adult hospital the next day and have surgery the day after. I awake in a recovery room and think I have died. Looking through foggy eyes, I see silver cabinets and beds. I don't want to be here; this isn't the kind of heaven I expected. I thrash around, pull out the needle in my arm and throw up, amidst nurses wrestling with me and telling me to stop.

I spend a week in the hospital recovering. My teacher, Mr. Killian, makes sure I keep up with my schoolwork. He visits me in the hospital and brings me my schoolwork, as well as a banner from my classmates. Mr. Killian rolls out the banner and holds it up for me to read. Colored pictures and names fill the paper. I feel like crying tears of joy. This banner is the best gift I've ever received. I return to school three or four days later.

I hope this feeling of happiness and warmth will carry me through the rest of the year. By the end of seventh grade, I have adjusted to the weekly allergy injections and frequent visits to my surgeon. As fall approaches, I feel another lump growing close to my large scar from my surgery. I can't believe this is happening again. By now, my breasts are developing. I sink onto my bed in our new house and place my arm across my face. I want to shrink inside myself and disappear. Basketball season is about to start. I do not want to miss any games. This season will be my best one yet as the top scorer playing three-on-three.

On my next visit to Dr. Graves, he feels the lump. I'm filled with dread. I feel as though a black curtain surrounds me. Like a thief, this tumor is going to rob me of basketball. When will my life ever be normal?

"I want to wait until after basketball season to have the tumor removed," I say.

I need this season. Playing sports helps me release anger and aggression—which I have in abundance. I need to pound things, to scream and holler in an acceptable way. Anger hangs just below the surface.

Surgery is scheduled for December 19, 1975—ten months since my last surgery. I will miss a few games, but it is better than the whole season. Before surgery, I hear snippets of conversations between my parents and my grandparents over the phone. I'm at the center of their conversations. Part of me doesn't want to know what is going on, while another part of me does. But I pick up enough information to realize that the number one cancer center in the United States wants me to fly there for a mastectomy. Four out of five major hospitals analyzed slides from my first surgery and believe I have a fibroadenoma, whereas the fifth hospital believes I have a precancerous tumor called a cystosarcoma phyllodes. When I put it all together, I tell Mom and Dad that I have no intention of traveling anywhere for surgery.

Dad nods. "I spoke with Dr. Graves," he says. "He told me he had four daughters and if you were his daughter, he would not have a mastectomy done. He thinks he just didn't get all of the first tumor."

Dr. Graves is one of the few doctors I trust and I know he has my best interest at heart. My second surgery goes without a hitch. I'm much more prepared this time around. I recover at home during Christmas break, and Stephen visits with me. Maybe now life will settle down.

# CHAPTER 12

At fourteen, I move to the high school Sunday school classroom. It's 1976. A new seminarian, Andy Khoury, is our teacher. He is a very large Lebanese man. My arms reach for the low ceiling as I stretch. We are given a basement room that has one window and one door and a lot of brick. All of us are taking stock of our new teacher and making judgments.

"I wonder where's he's from," I whisper to a friend. "He doesn't look cool, like our last seminarian."

"He sure is a big man," she whispers back.

The teacher drops a Bible on the floor. *Smack!* Heads jerk up and yawns stop midway. The sound echoes to a muted silence.

"What does the Bible mean to you?" he asks in a booming voice.

Most of us look at each other to see who will break the silence. Andy urges us to throw out anything that comes to mind. None of us wants to look dumb.

"It's the word of God?" someone squeaks out.

"What else?" he says in a challenging tone.

"A book about God?" another teenager manages.

My pulse begins to slow down as I wipe my palms on my slacks. Who *is* this person? I can't believe he threw a Bible on the floor.

"The Bible is not about the book itself," Andy explains, "but about what's on the inside."

All eyes are on him now, but with less judgment.

*Huh, maybe he's cooler than I thought.*

I grimace as my brother Brandon makes a sarcastic remark.

"Do you throw all your books on the floor?"

Neither of us is happy that we are in the same class. We are oil and water, and I'm often embarrassed by my brother. Other than our parents, our love of motorcycles is about the only thing we share in common. He has no interest in me and I am hurt by that. I go to his wrestling matches and cheer him on with all I have, but Brandon acts as if I don't exist.

I don't like that my parents treat Brandon as special because he's short and left-handed. In competition, my teams always won and his didn't. He decided to quit baseball and make money by starting a lawn-cutting business. The schism between us grew wider.

I jump in with both feet after Brandon's comment. "Can't you see he's trying to make a point?" I ask through clenched teeth.

My body tenses as I argue with him and Andy calls a truce. *Brandon is so immature and stupid! Why did I get him as my brother?!* Maybe Andy will protect me from Brandon's meanness. I glance up to see Andy watching me. He winks. My heart melts some and I begin to look forward to Sundays.

At home, Dad seems to be more absent than present. Sometimes I see his car lights coming up the driveway as I look through my curtains late at night. Then I let my breath out without having realized I was holding it. Those are the good nights. Even though he misses dinner and watching TV with us, he still comes home to us. On the nights he stays out, I hear Mom cry. Anger floods my heart. I feel like a rubber band stretched to the point of breaking.

The next day, I find Dad in the kitchen pouring coffee.

"Hey, Dad. I miss being with you."

"I miss you too, Steph," he says. "I'm real busy at the studio. I've got to work tomorrow too."

"On Sunday?"

"Yes. I'm helping some students get ready for a competition."

I walk out of the kitchen with a heavy heart. I hope I haven't pushed him further away.

Sundays with Andy become a haven. I feel cared for by him. Brandon and I argue any time we're together, but I don't feel as alone. Outside of church and school, I'm on my own much of the time. Mom is distant and sad. My friends, who are Catholic, don't seem to struggle within their families. They lack the ears to hear me, and I don't want to make myself stand out any more than I already do by not being Catholic. I scoop up Andy's interest in me like ice cream.

I step into Sunday school and see Andy standing inside.

"I'm looking forward to hanging out with you and your family after church," he says.

Andy and his wife, Maureen, live up the mountain in Sewanee. I'm glad it's too far for him to go home for lunch on Sundays. Instead, Andy remains in town and stays with one of the youth group families until it's time for our evening youth gathering.

"Me too," I reply. "Maybe we can shoot some hoops."

"Sounds like fun."

Back home, I look out my bedroom window. I rock on the balls of my feet. Then I see Andy's two-door, dull green Chevrolet pull into our driveway. I feel like jumping up and down with excitement. We play basketball and throw a softball around in the backyard. His athleticism surprises me. I love having someone to play sports with me. Most of the time I shoot hoops by myself or throw a softball against a pitch-back. Brandon doesn't hang around and wouldn't play with me anyway, so I get Andy to myself.

The next Sunday, I find my body warming in his presence. I crave attention and he gives it freely. Andy makes a point to speak to me as soon as I walk into the cave-like classroom and looks at me when he teaches the lesson. I know he does the same thing with my friends, but Andy does it more with me. He makes a point of touching my arm or giving me a big hug when he sees me.

Just before the summer, Andy invites me to spend a week with him and Maureen in Sewanee. Mom agrees to let me go, but I have another month of softball to play first. As excited as I am at being with Andy, I feel anxious too. What will I do with these two adults? I want to bring my motorcycle. I don't like being away from home. What if I don't like their food? Will they let me drink Coca-Cola? What if I get bored? Round and round my thoughts go. Andy says I can't bring my motorcycle.

After softball season comes to an end, I stuff my fourteen-year-old fears as I climb in the back of their car after church. My anxieties follow me in as I set my suitcase next to me. I'm more of a homebody. I never did well at camps—even day camps. The front end of the car dips as Andy climbs behind the steering wheel. Maureen slides in the front seat next to him. My long hair flies as my eyes watch the sparse houses zip by as we head towards the mountain. The smell of diesel fuel fills my nostrils. I can do a week with them. Maybe it won't be so bad. But an underlying dread remains with me.

The University of the South's campus in Sewanee fills my vision as we slow down, and I am struck by its beauty.

"You live here?"

"Not far from here," Andy says. "The stonework is called Gothic architecture."

I've never seen anything like it. It reminds me of a medieval castle or something like it. "Wow."

Andy smiles. "Most of the buildings at Sewanee are made of the same material. You'll see more when I take you on a tour after lunch."

Andy steers the car toward their house and turns off the main road. As we pull into their short, part concrete, part gravel driveway, I try to hide my disappointment. Their house is tiny. There are several housing units like theirs, each with the same matching stones as the campus buildings.

The interior of the house is unremarkable, with a tiny kitchen, small sitting area, and one bedroom and one bathroom. I gulp as I look around and wonder where I will sleep. Andy's eyes meet mine.

"Don't worry, we have a rollaway bed for you to sleep on."

The air rushes from my lungs as I drop my shoulders.

While Maureen makes lunch, Andy tells me more about the campus. "I want to show you where Maureen and I first lived when we moved here. It's at the convent."

"Episcopalians have nuns?"

"Yes. Some of them may have been married at one time too."

After lunch, the two of us climb back in their car with me in the front seat. Andy turns down a country road. He covers my hand with his. My whole body relaxes. Finally, someone cares about me and is choosing to spend time with me. I ache to be held and comforted. I feel like crying as the loneliness slips away. My worries at home move to the back of my mind.

"How're you feeling?" Andy asks.

"I'm good."

"What's 'good' mean?"

"I mean, I'm happy to be here. With you. You seem to understand me and care about me. My parents don't seem to be interested in me anymore, but you do."

"Steph, you know they care about you. They're having troubles right now. I'm glad I can offer you comfort during this time."

"Do you think they will be okay?" I whisper. My heart drops and I feel my hand release some sweat. I didn't realize I'd said that out loud. I hold my breath as if Andy has the inside story on my parents' relationship.

"Only God knows the answer to that. We can pray for them."

He smiles at me and squeezes my hand. I'm more and more glad I came to visit with them. And it's only the first day. I have a whole week of someone spending time with me.

The past two years have been one big roller coaster. I became an asthmatic filled with allergies. I had major surgery—twice. I moved into a new house and met my birth father. Now, my stepdad is slipping away. Our family is unraveling at record speed.

A part of me feels I belong to Andy in some way—even before he brought me to this mountain.

# CHAPTER 13

It's June 2020 and I wake up feeling wet with a strong urge to pee. Damn. I hurry to the bathroom while trying not to drip on the floor. I sit on the cold toilet seat and empty my bladder. I crease my brow in the dark and rub my face. What's going on? This is the third time in the last month I haven't made it to the toilet in time. Up until May, I hadn't been sleeping well. Now I'm sleeping like a bear in hibernation. I don't know what's going on with my body.

I open my bedroom door the next morning. Mike and the pups are sitting on the couch. A hint of the glow from his iPad shines on his face.

"Good morning, babe." He smiles at me.

"Good morning." I come behind Mike and hug him for a moment—always wary of the virus. "It happened again last night. I nearly wet the bed."

"Did you have any stinging or burning?

"No. Nothing else seems to be different except my waking up and needing to pee."

My mind tells me I should feel embarrassed, but I refuse to cooperate.

Mike reassures me that it's probably nothing to worry about, but I decide to talk about it with Brooke during our session tomorrow.

After I wash my sheets, I sit at my desk with the pups asleep on the newly made bed behind me. I wonder if writing my memoir is causing a physical reaction. Thinking and writing about my experience with Andy is pushing me back to a time I'd like to forget. I take a deep breath and begin typing the words that come to me. I know if I don't write about this episode now, I will continue to be bogged down by my past. Even though it hurts, I believe I must go through this pain in order to heal.

Writing allows me to see myself through the eyes of a young girl and now as an adult. Reliving these experiences is hard, but this process means I feel what I felt as a child and the adult in me gets to hug her and let her know everything will be all right. What I felt at that time and how I expressed it fell short of the truth because I stuffed my feelings into that space in my heart. Now I can hold the mirror up and see two different images. I feel power in that, and that's where the healing comes in. I'm not rewriting history—I'm understanding my reactions and my actions more. I'm guessing my enuresis is from the pressure my subconscious is experiencing.

I shift in my chair. A dream I had a few weeks ago keeps creeping into my mind. I stretch my arms above my head while rain beats down outside the windows. The dream takes hold and consumes my thoughts.

I am out of town with a friend. We are in the parking lot of a hotel where we will be spending the night. I look across the lot and see our youth group from church, with my goddaughter, Lacy, in their midst. I squint my eyes and see Andy joining them. What's he doing? Get away from her!

Some of the youth drift over to us. They are excited about their time together for the weekend. I tell them to stay away from that man as I point to Andy. Lacy asks if they can just talk to him.

"No! Do not talk to him."

We separate. I join my friend behind this huge, futuristic-looking dump truck. Inside the back of the truck are large steel containers filled with suitcases. As the monstrous vehicle crosses the parking lot, the rooms unzip and the truck shoots out the suitcases automatically, one by one, into the appropriate rooms. Immediately I think about George Orwell's book *1984* and how it affected me when I read it in 1980. I feel a sense of dread about leaving Andy with the youth group. How did he get here in the first place? I want him to disappear.

I prop my elbows on my desk and think about my relationship with Andy through the lens of a movie. According to an article I found on the internet about the stages of grooming, it is clear I was groomed: targeting the child, gaining the child's and caregiver's trust, filling a need, isolating the child, sexualizing the relationship, and maintaining control. I fit the victim's mold to a T.

The next day, I join Brooke for our teletherapy session. After greeting each other, I tell her that I think I'm dealing with an issue related to my writing.

"What's going on?"

"I've wet my bed several times over the past month or so. It's not much, but still. I've never experienced this issue before. I'm writing about Andy and how he groomed me. I think that might be the cause of the problem."

"Have you talked with your gynecologist?"

"Not yet, but I should rule out the physical component."

Then I tell Brooke about my dream and wait for her reaction.

"Your yelling at the youth group to stay away sounds to me like you're finding your voice."

"That's what it felt like. I knew he wouldn't bother me anymore, but I didn't want him to try anything with them—especially my goddaughter."

As I speak, my hands tense in my lap.

"Sometimes I wonder if I'll ever be free of my tortured dreams and rewinding my past mistakes. It's like I'm searching for answers in the darkest part of my mind. If you could do a cutaway of my life, you would see all the graces and gifts of my present on the surface. Go deeper, and the worst parts of my life shine in red."

"You're doing a lot of work, Steph."

"It's not easy. I can't wait to get past the parts with Andy in them."

"And you will, Steph."

I take this reassurance in. Yes, I will get past this part, and I will be healthier because of it. I want to stop having accidents—but it's a small price to pay.

# CHAPTER 14

Andy holds my hand all the way back to his and Maureen's home.

"Will you throw ball with me?" I ask.

"Sure."

We gather our gloves and return to the broken asphalt in front. Once again, I'm amazed at how hard Andy can throw a softball. *Thwump* goes my glove as the ball smashes into it. My arm throws a punch as well. I raise my arm above my head and step forward, straightening my elbow before releasing the ball. I could do this forever.

The smell of macaroni and cheese seeps through the screen door. Pots and pans rattle in the kitchen. My stomach growls.

"Let's get ready for supper," Andy says.

I stretch my arms above my head and bend to the ground and stand back up. With my glove in the crook of my arm, I follow Andy through the door. Fried fish, green beans, and mac and cheese sit on the counter in the kitchen. I hurry to the bathroom. The water feels cool on my warm, dirty hands. The bar of soap slides into the sink. I put it back and head to the kitchen. We bow our heads at the table.

"Father," Andy prays, "thank You for this meal and for Steph's time with us. Amen."

I gobble up my serving. After dinner, the kitchen sink fills with bubbles as Maureen scrubs our plates.

"Why don't you come sit with me," Andy says.

The cushion on the couch sinks under him. My body falls into him while his meaty arm reaches around me and pulls me closer. Dishes clink together across the tiny room. A pleasant smell comes off Andy's body, and my body joins his when he pulls my arm across his large waist. I want to melt into him but am watchful of Maureen. Andy kisses the top of my head. I wonder what she thinks of him as he cradles me.

*Is this snuggling okay? Andy's a seminarian who is loved and respected by the people at our church.*

"Everything's going to be all right," Andy softly whispers to me. "Just relax."

My shoulders drop down and I allow myself to trust him. Everyone else does.

At bedtime, Maureen goes into their bedroom while Andy helps me get ready for bed. I hear the squeaky wheels of the rollaway bed coming towards me. We lift the sheets high in the air and watch as they flutter down to the bed. I look up to see Andy's hooded eyes smiling at me. As I climb in, he leans down and kisses me on the lips. My heart speeds up and I feel tingly all over. *Only my dad and grandmother kiss me on the lips. Is Andy trying to act like a dad?* Despite my thoughts, I sleep well. Morning comes early.

Each day we throw ball together, but when we are alone, we hold hands and kiss. I am confused, but my thirst for attention accepts all of his gestures. I allow myself to let go of wrong or right thoughts. I'm tired of feeling the burden of responsibility. This big, kindhearted man wants to take care of my needs and I let him. He seems to love me in a special way.

Later in the week at bedtime, Andy tucks me in, then sits beside me. A small light from the kitchen stove barely reaches us. I sit up, expecting another kiss. Instead, he undoes the top snaps on my pajama top. I hold my breath. *Touch me.* His plump hand reaches through the gap and touches my left breast. As his fingers lightly touch my scar, a sound escapes him. Warmth flows down to my belly. He withdraws his hand and stiffens. With a shake of his head, he walks to his bedroom.

*What just happened? Please don't leave. Why did you stop? Did I do something wrong?* It's as if he burned his fingers. Did he go too far? What is going on? I feel let down.

Soon, sounds come through the thin walls. I hear their bed moving and noises coming from Maureen. Are they having sex? Was I the warm-up? I want out of here. I hate him. Lying in bed, I want to cry but the tears don't come.

I wake up feeling angry. *Don't mess with me.*

Andy pretends he is happy and life is good. "Do you want to spend the day with me at Taylor's Hardware Store?" he asks. "The boss is on vacation, and I told him I would fill in. You can drive us over there."

I swallow the bribe. I love to drive. Last month, my grandmother bought herself a brand-new 1976 Cadillac. "Stephie," she says through the phone, "how 'bout I bring the car to your house, and you can take it for a drive? I thought we would do it while your mom is at work."

"Grandmom, you don't need to do that. You know I'm just fourteen years old."

"I was driving my daddy's manual car on the farm when I was twelve. You will be just fine."

My grandmother trusts me. I have several hours of joy picking up my softball friends and driving around because their parents allowed them to ride with me. Adults are a mystery to me. They make rules and then break them.

I slide into the driver's side of Andy's car. I move the seat way up. My bottom gets lost in a sinkhole. Even though my motorcycle license won't help me if I'm pulled over, I have it on me. As I back out of the driveway, my heart rate speeds up and I smile. My hands relax on the steering wheel. Andy doesn't offer any instructions. He trusts my driving skills too. When we were younger, Dad let Brandon and me sit on his lap and drive home from Cleveland, Tennessee, back to Chattanooga. I feel like a pro.

As we enter the hardware store, I gaze at the tall ceilings and large glass windows. I feel swallowed up in the empty space. I wrap my arms around myself and remember what happened last night. I tighten my grip and feel anger well up again. Andy sits on a stool by the cash register while I stay near the back.

The silver bell rings above the front door. Andy's voice bellows out a hello. "Steph, come here and let me introduce you to Charlie. Charlie can fix anything that's broken."

I want to hide behind the cold, hard tools. Instead, I drag my feet toward their voices. Andy pulls me to him and introduces me to Charlie. Andy squeezes me in a way that feels like he owns me. I smile and shake hands with Charlie.

"We're going to have lunch at Shenanigan's across the street," Andy tells him. "Can you join us?"

"Nah. I got to get going on this project."

I slip away from them as soon as I can. I want to go home. Today is my last day here. I will avoid Andy as best I can until we leave.

The next morning, I pack up and we head down the mountain towards Chattanooga. As we pull into Grace Episcopal Church's parking lot, I open the door and leap out. A few friends are also arriving for Sunday school. I run to them as if they are lifesavers. I take a deep breath and know I will keep what happened with Andy a secret in my heart space. But now it's time for class with Andy as our teacher.

# CHAPTER 15

High school begins in a few weeks, and I want to ride my motorcycle as much as I can. As a fourteen-year-old, my license extends only to a seven-mile radius from my house, but I feel reckless. I don't know who I am. I left Andy's home with more questions than answers. I want to be loved, yet I don't know what that means. What is acceptable and what is not? Maybe a long ride will help me feel better.

The day is hot and humid. Sweat seeps from my scalp as soon as I pull my bike out of the garage. My iridescent initials shine on the orange gas tank. I kick-start the two-wheeled machine and head for I-75 South. To hell with the invisible seven-mile fence. As soon as I merge onto the highway, I feel my worries slough off. Because my bike is too small to be on the freeway, I stay in the right-hand lane.

Worry melts away. Freedom surrounds me. Wildness. Inside my darkened helmet, I smile and yell "Ahhhhhh." I'm a caged animal, released. My slouched body straightens. I belong on this road. Adults have given me too much responsibility—*Stephanie can handle this, she's strong*—so I might as well pretend I'm one of them. But what if I don't want to be strong? What if I just want to be taken care of? Except that I trust someone who is supposed to be a man of the cloth and I'm not sure he is who people think he is or who I think he is. I throttle the engine to go as fast as it can.

I exit in East Ridge and decide to turn around and head back home. My body is slick with baby oil and perspiration. My cutoff shorts and bikini top allow me to tan while I ride. My long hair whips at my back. I smell cut grass, exhaust fumes, and diesel. As I look around from my perch, I notice an eighteen-wheeler coming my way in the fast lane. All of a sudden, my small Honda XL-100 bike is sucked into the huge truck. I see my reflection in its chrome wheel covers. My palms moisten and hold tight to the handlebar grips. I may die. I feel my body begin to shake.

What an awful way to go. I can't imagine how it will feel. Will I flatten like a pancake? No one will know that it's me. *Help!* I didn't know this could happen. Nobody knows where I am. Will I be missed? I can almost reach out and touch the hot steel.

I'm not ready to die. I want to make a difference in this world. I need more time. I don't want to just cease to exist.

I lean hard to the right, using all my ninety-pound body weight. I feel the magnet between me and the giant truck starting to release its grip. My motorcycle breaks away and swings to the right like a rocket. I grip my handlebars and brake hard so I won't hit the gravel or guardrail. As soon as my wheels come to a stop, I slide off my bike and remove my helmet. I feel like kissing the hot rocks. I've never been so happy to be standing on the ground. My heart beats like a hammer. I feel woozy too. In spite of my recklessness, God has given me another chance. I return home and fall asleep on my bed, oil and all.

A week later, my parents talk with me together about high school.

"Steph," Dad begins, "your mom and I think Girls' Preparatory School is where you need to be. We want you to have the best education."

*GPS??* "I don't want to go there. I am *not* wearing those dresses. I want to be with boys *and* girls. All my St. Stephen's friends will be going to the other private school, City Private School. That's where I'd rather go. *Please.* It's a good school too."

I look from one parent to the other as Dad sighs. I hope I'm not being too difficult. Dad's home tonight and I don't want to push him away, but school is important to me.

"Plus, Brandon can take me to school since it's only a few miles from his school."

"Okay, we'll talk about it some more and let you know what we decide."

I go to my room, shut the door, and flop on my bed. I run the conversation through my mind. My childhood hippo collapses in my arms as I pull it close. It's limp from all the hugging I've given it. But, wow, I found my voice today. I stood up for myself because I want to be with my friends.

The smell of chicken and cream of mushroom soup find its way to my room. "Time for dinner," Mom yells from the kitchen.

Dad, Brandon, and I make our way to the kitchen. All four plates are set on the table. I take a deep breath in anticipation of Mom and Dad's decision. Steam rises from the rice. Mom adds the leftover soup on top. I smile. It's rare to have all four of us eating together. Dad's always at his dance studio. My parents seem to be holding on by a thread.

As Dad slathers butter on his bread, he clears his throat.

"Steph, your mom and I have decided to let you attend CPS. We think GPS is a better school, but CPS has a good reputation."

"Yay! I'll get to be with my friends. Thank you!"

Brandon wipes his mouth and keeps on eating. His indifference slides off me. I feel warm on the inside. Changing schools will be hard enough on me; now, though, I will have familiar faces to help make the transition easier. My softball friend, Mary, will be going there too.

I scoot my chair back and get up and hug my parents. They have no idea how much this decision means to me. I need some stability in my life—something they're no longer offering me. It's like we're four individuals instead of a family of four.

I overheard Mom on the phone the other day, talking to Dad. "Tom, why can't you come home earlier?"

I don't know what he said, but she frowned and took a deep breath. I went outside. My stomach felt so tight it was hard to catch my breath.

After tonight's dinner, I help clean up the kitchen. When I return to my room, I flop down on my beanbag chair to think. It seems that Mom and Dad don't want the same things anymore.

Sometimes, when my clock reads midnight, I see his headlights as he heads up the driveway. I pop my head out my door and see Mom's bedroom lights still on. I slip back into bed before Dad comes upstairs. I hear his hands brush against the hall walls as he steadies himself.

Mom seems sad most of the time now. She cries more and appears frantic to hold on to him. Her sadness becomes my sadness. My chest hurts. I hold on tight to my stuffed animal. I don't like seeing Mom this way and I hope Dad knows we still need him. I know I do.

Staring at the ceiling, I think about when Brandon and I were sent to Sioux Falls, South Dakota, to visit Don and Joanna. I was thirteen and Brandon was fifteen. He couldn't wait to spend time with Don. I did not want to, but Mom and Dad made me go.

"Steph," Dad said, "it's a chance to get to know each other."

"I. Don't. Want. To. Go. Can't you come too?"

"No, Steph. This trip is for you and Brandon and Don."

As soon as our plane lands and we walk into the little room off the gate, we look around for Don. We've only met him once.

"Where is he?" Brandon asks. He starts fidgeting with his clothes.

"It's okay," I say. "There's a pay phone right by the door. I have ten cents. We'll be fine."

A few minutes later, Don walks through the door. He smiles and tells us we need to go to baggage claim. Brandon relaxes again.

As we leave the airport, Don tells us that we're going to be camping. "Your parents said you like to do that. Some friends of ours and their children are already at the campsite."

I slide down the backseat and the car closes in on me. My palms begin to sweat.

The ride takes forever.

"Here we are," Don says. "We have tents for all you kids."

My breath leaves me as my heart pounds against my ribs. Tears well up. I want to go home. Brandon heads to a picnic table filled with teenagers. Where can I go? Don walks towards a camper. I stand still outside the car, then see Joanna heading my way. I hope she's as nice as she seemed when we met earlier in the year.

"Hey, Steph," Joanna greets me. "Are you okay? Do you want to take a walk?" I feel paralyzed. She reaches for my hand. "Come with me."

My body shakes as I keep pace beside her. I don't know these people. They are strangers to me—including Brandon. My ears feel stopped up.

"How was your flight?"

I can't seem to answer her. She squeezes my hand. This trip is worse than when I went to a YMCA day camp and clung to the director all day.

Joanna walks over to a girl sitting near the camper. "I want you to meet my daughter, Michelle." Michelle and I say hello to each other.

Most of the time we're in Sioux Falls, I cry and refuse to eat. If Joanna and Michelle hadn't been so nice to me, I don't know what I would have done. I had begged not to come here and then I begged to go home early. I want to be with my dad—the one who raised me. The other one can have Brandon.

Jumping out of my beanbag chair, I shake off these memories, grab the phone off the hook, and make sure no one is on it. I call my friend Mary and tell her I will be going to CPS too. She's as excited as I am. We talk about what sports we will play together. My heart feels lighter as I dream about our new high school.

# CHAPTER 16

It's the Fourth of July 2020, and our sons and their friends are here. We are celebrating the holiday as well as the upcoming move to Hawaii for Michael, our older son. Like balloons exploding, the sound of fireworks ignites all around us. *Boom!* My gaze turns to our sons and their friends. They stand apart from each other as they social distance on our dock. Such a fitting send-off for Michael. My heart bursts with the possibilities for him.

I lean into Michael and ask again if he is excited to be moving to Hawaii.

"I am," he says. "I can't wait." He smiles as more fireworks light up the sky.

I slip back into my hammock and take a deep breath. Next year, Mike and I hope to be living on this property. Building our home here may start as early as this fall. I wrap my arms around myself and feel so blessed. I love my family and marvel at how lucky I am.

There were times when I wondered if I deserved a healthy family. I dreamed, but not with a lot of confidence, of having a *Brady Bunch* family minus the mixed family dynamics. I learned as much as I could about life through books and observation. I prayed to have moments like these tonight long before I met Mike. Even though I always felt love from my mom, I knew there was another way I wanted to be as a parent. I *know* I'm not as obsessive as she was about having a spotless house. Win!

I recognize Mom did the best she could with what she had. Her parents pushed her into marriage when she had just turned sixteen. Instead of enjoying her teenage years, she married, quit high school, and kept an eye on her husband, who had an affair within the first year of their marriage. Don was in the Navy and stationed in Virginia. Mom moved in with him, got a job, had two kids, and tried to make the marriage work. She supported him through medical school—only to have him leave when he finished his residency. Mom made many sacrifices for us.

Today, we talk every day. I love her so much. I gaze at my own family and feel pride and happiness. I'm going to miss Michael, but I'm so happy for him.

The wind rocks me in my snuggly cocoon. I think back on my life and how different the lives of our two boys are from what mine was. Home-educating them from kindergarten to high school kept us close; we were together twenty-four seven. As hard as it was, I would do it again. I look at these two young men. I wasn't able to keep them from everything not good and whole, thanks to the internet, but I tried to cushion their lives while encouraging independence.

*Ka-boom*! Mike jumps back as he sends his own burst of explosion and color into the sky. *Bam, bam, bam* come the aftereffects onto the canopy above our dock. Everyone dives under the dock roof to avoid getting hit. Nervous laughter fills the air.

Hands go to ears as Mike lights another rocket. It feels like we're in a war zone. I make sure I'm completely protected from the remnants of the bursts. Now that I know what to expect, I cover my ears and watch the night sky. I don't want to be anywhere else in the world but here. My best friend sits in a chair in front of me, while one of her daughters sits in the back of our docked boat. The other daughter is mingling with the guys. The two of them are our goddaughters.

I thank God for this night. Deaths from the pandemic continue to rise and I know people who have died from the virus. Tonight, though, I need a break. I hold my family and friends close and enjoy these last moments with Michael. I push pause on my past.

A few days later, the three of us drive the 125-mile route to the Atlanta airport. Michael and Mike talk in the front seat while I listen from the back. My open palms rest on my lap. I look down at them and realize what I am doing metaphorically with our twenty-seven-year-old son: I am releasing him. As we pull up to the curb for Delta Air Lines, Michael leaps out to get his bag. I join him on the sidewalk. We hug before he turns away towards his next adventure. *Lord, please take care of our son. Thank You for Michael.*

Mike and I return home after a quick stop at our younger son's apartment in Atlanta. I release the pause button as I watch the news. More than two hundred thousand people have died from Covid-19. Mike sits across from me, wearing his mask, as we gaze at the numbers. I feel my muscles tighten. I don't want to be one of the numbers. I offer another prayer. *Please, Lord, keep us safe. I lift up those who have died from this virus. Thank You for Your many gifts.*

I remain quarantined by staying at home in Toccoa or by sitting on the new dock on our lake property.

My mind returns to my past to face other vulnerable times in my life. I want to heal from the internal virus deep inside me. Past abuse has left me feeling isolated. I shouldn't feel this way anymore, but I do. When will my thoughts stay in the present? Why does my past trauma still plague me today? Most mornings I wake up feeling exhausted and sad. I live such a sweet life, yet my body stays on high alert.

Today as I scan Facebook, I stop and stare at an advertisement, something I don't normally do. It's about how our nervous system gets tricked into thinking trauma is happening in the present.

What? I'm not the only person who does this? Seriously?

# CHAPTER 17

It's September of 1976 and I'm riding in the backseat of my brother's blue, two-door 1968 Mustang for the first day of school. From the radio, Boston's "More Than a Feeling" blares through the back speakers as Brandon's cigarette smoke flies in my face through his cracked window. We pick up my friend Debbie at a gas station and she rides in the front. Conversation is minimal.

"Brandon, turn down the music," I yell. "It's hurting my ears."

He's in a good mood. His fingers reach for the volume knob, twist it to the left, and I breathe a sigh of relief. My ears still throb inside. Once we stop at CPS, I hurry to get out of the car after Debbie. I'm already dreading this new weekday ritual. The twenty-minute ride seems much longer—even with Brandon's speeding.

The bell rings. Plaid skirts, white shirts, and ties flash by as students rush to their classrooms. I tuck my skirt under me as I slide into my desk and look around to see if any of the faces are familiar. I recognize a few from Missionary Ridge and others from playing basketball. I know I'll be all right. It will take time for me to adjust to my new school, but I can see that sports and friends will get me through the year.

At church, Andy continues to teach Sunday school and work with the youth. I like the special treatment I get from him, but I avoid being alone with him. I want his love without his touching my body. Since Maureen didn't say anything about his kissing me when I stayed with them, maybe that's all right. The rest of it feels wrong, though, and I don't trust him to just kiss me.

Freshman year flies by. Months later, Andy joins me and my family for Easter lunch after church, but Maureen returns to Sewanee instead of joining us. We go to a restaurant near Chickamauga Dam. At the long table in a private room, Andy seats himself beside me. My grandparents, my uncle and his wife, and the rest of my family scrape their chairs against the floor as they find their places. I have a pit in my stomach. My right leg begins to jiggle.

All of us are dressed to the nines in our Easter best. Our voices fill the room. We have a talking family. My uncle's voice competes with the others as he tells stories from his medical residency and laughter replaces the buzzing of conversation. I bounce my leg even more under the table. I feel like a fraud in front of my family with this man sitting beside me.

Andy clamps his hand on my knee under the table.

"Where're you going?" Andy asks and winks.

"What do you mean?"

"You're moving your knee so fast it's like you're trying to get somewhere."

*If you only knew. My insides are a mess. I'm afraid of you. I don't like being with you in front of my family. What if they find out about us?*

I stop fidgeting. As soon as I forget about it, though, my leg seems to bounce on its own.

Once again, Andy pushes my knee down with one hand.

"You need to calm down," he says.

"I am calm."

"Your leg says differently."

I want this meal to end so I can go home and be away from Andy.

Dessert finally comes. "Do you mind if I drive Stephanie home?" Andy asks my mom.

I cringe inside. *Please* say no.

"Sure. That's fine."

*Nooooo.*

I wipe my mouth and follow him to his car. As Andy opens the door for me, my legs want to run. What is this? A date? He smiles and shoves himself behind the steering wheel. The tick-tick-ticking turn signal is the only sound in the car. Andy turns right on Amnicola Highway towards Chickamauga Dam. His hand reaches for mine. Within a minute, he turns left onto a road that ends at a large empty parking lot.

My heart rate takes off while I rub my moist hands on my slacks. He turns the engine off, and with veiled eyes he reaches for me and begins kissing me. A part of me responds to his affection, while the other part prays a car will pull in. Even though it's warm outside, I feel cold. I sit ramrod straight as his hand goes to my crotch and gently rubs against my pants. I stare out the window, unable to focus on any one thing. My legs go numb as my sexual instincts betray me. I feel moist down there. For a brief moment, I want to push his hand against me.

My body's response confuses my understanding of right and wrong. I know what he's doing isn't right and yet I want to be touched. It's the wrong person and wrong time in my life. Why does it have to feel so good? Just like when I was seven years old . . .

A sigh escapes from Andy as he turns to face forward, his hands to himself. Nothing is said, but I can feel him struggling with desire. It's as if he wants more of me but another voice tells him to stop. I'm grateful he is listening to that voice. He puts the car in reverse and drives back to the highway. Even though the ride home is quiet, my brain is on hyperdrive. My leg begins to fidget again.

I can't believe Andy touched me down there—albeit through clothes. I know he feels in charge of me somehow, but he has stepped across a line. Kissing feels safe; this other thing is something forbidden and altogether wrong. I know he shouldn't have done it, but if I tell my parents, I don't know if they'll believe me and I don't know what would happen to Andy. It's all too much. I open the space inside my heart and tuck away another secret. I must keep myself away from Andy.

Summer comes just in time. I soak up the normality that the season affords: Things will slow down at church and heat up on the ballfield. Playing fast-pitch will keep me occupied. At home, Brandon stays in the basement or is out on dates. He is a like a houseguest as Mom and Dad continue to drift apart.

Softball is good for me because on the field I'm in charge. As a catcher, I hold the game in my hands when we play defense.

We are in our final tournament of the season. This one is for the Elsie Snyder Championship. Betsey, a runner built tough as steel, is on second. She holds track records, even with her solid frame. If we can keep her from scoring, we'll win.

I wiggle two fingers in the air. "Two down," I yell to my teammates.

Fans yell from the stands as our pitcher throws a strike. I pound my glove with my fist after I throw the ball back. The next pitch comes in hard and fast. *Ping!* The batter sends the ball to left field. Betsey takes off from second base like a horse coming out of its starting gate. My heart rate accelerates as I see the outfielder stop the ball and rear back with her arm to throw it to me.

Betsey's speed has her crossing third as the ball comes sailing toward home. I begin to see both Betsey and the ball in slow motion. Betsey's facial muscles are churning; she is determined to get home before the ball reaches me.

The ball hits my glove a half second before Betsey's head-on dive drives into me. My pigtails fly in the air as I'm sent into a backwards flip. With my mask askew and dirt flying around me, I hold up my glove with the ball still in it. The fans roar and clap as my coaches run to me. The umpire yells, "Out!"

"Yogi, are you all right?" C.E. asks.

Barney checks me over with a big smile on his face. "Yog, next time pick up the plate and hand it to Betsey," he says.

My teammates surround me as I hug my best friend, Waddie, the outfielder. We smile and let our breath out. Catching the ball and tagging Betsey out is something I want to remember for the rest of my life. I promise myself that I will never forget that feeling.

Our parents take to the field, shouting and hugging us. My boyfriend looks amazed. I had thought I was the only one who needed this win. I was wrong. We all needed it.

# CHAPTER 18

It's the summer of 1977. The rules of my motorcycle license disintegrate by convenience. Even though I have no intention of taking my bike on the highway again, I ride it to softball practices using alternate routes. My parents seem too distracted to notice I ride past the seven-mile limit. Today, staying within the limit, I pull on my orange helmet, kick-start the bike, and head over to the home of my coach Barney and his wife, Brenda.

*Ding-dong.* I push the doorbell and run back to my bike.

"Hey, Barney and Brenda," I yell. "Wanna see what I just learned to do?"

Their bodies fill the door.

"Watch this."

I crank my bike, then rev up the engine. My body vibrates as the *ning, ning, ning, ning, ning* sound of the engine fills the air. I grip the throttle and twist my wrist. At the peak of the revolutions per minute, I pop the clutch.

The front wheel lifts in the air. I smile as my heart quickens. But then, like a lion roaring on its hind legs, my bike stands straight up. *Oh, shit.* I hear the fender scraping the road but can't get my legs around the back blinkers to steady myself. Somehow, both wheels find the ground again as I try to hang on. My right hand is glued to the throttle. A cul-de-sac looms ahead. The bike and I wobble our way to the circle. Loose gravel kicks the front wheel out from under me as the crash bar drags on the pavement—along with my left knee. Pain shoots through me as my hand releases the gas. I fall, then jump from the ground and pick up the motorcycle.

"Yogi, are you all right?" Barney yells. He and Brenda jog to me.

"I think my bike's okay. Just a few scrapes on the crash bar."

"We don't care about the motorcycle," Brenda says. "We care about how *you* are."

Blood seeps from my skinned knee. Rocks and debris are embedded in the wounds. Feeling like an idiot, I want to disappear. Barney pushes the bike back toward their house. In the kitchen, Brenda cleans up my knee and hands me some water. My armpits are sticky with sweat.

"That was quite a wheelie," says Barney.

Water shoots from my mouth onto the floor. He always knows how to make me laugh.

"I guess I overdid it. I wanted to show off."

The weight of embarrassment lifts and is replaced by love. My wheelie days are over. I doubt I'll ever challenge the power of my motorcycle again.

Sophomore year begins. My parents refuse to allow me to ride my motorcycle to school, so Brandon continues as chauffeur for Debbie and me. He's seventeen and I'm fifteen, but he feels like a stranger to me. I watch him tap his cigarette between his fingers. I glance at the back of Debbie's blonde head and wonder if her four siblings are anything like my brother.

Basketball tryouts find me sitting on the gym's stairs. The scabs on my knee from the bike accident are healing, but I don't feel like participating. Coach McCarthy and I don't get along. We're like rams butting heads.

"Stephanie, if you want to play this year," Coach McCarthy yells, "I have to see what you can do. Today."

I need someone like Barney to sit beside me and talk me through my feelings. I drop my head onto my knees and look at the bottom step. Debbie and Mary, along with the other girls, dribble balls up and down the court. The smell of sweat reaches me. The squeaks of high-tops bounce off the gym walls. In high school, girls' basketball is played on the full court. Asthma prevents me from keeping up and strips me of the chance to be the top scorer. I want to join in the tryouts, but pride leads me outside to the car.

A few months later, friends invite me to try out for volleyball. It's our second year of playing and Coach Williams seems as excited as we are.

"Salmon, huh?" Coach Williams says to me. "I think I'll call you Fish instead. You look like a fish."

"I already have a nickname. It's Yogi, for Yogi Berra."

"Nah. You're Fish to me."

We play on the basketball court, which eats up my knee pads. I spend most of my time on my knees or diving across the gym floor. I love this new challenge.

One day, when Mom picks me up from school, I notice her wet cheeks.

"What's wrong?"

"Your daddy left us."

My body trembles, but I plaster a fake smile. *I need to be strong for her.* "We'll be all right. Dad's not been home much anyway."

My insides boil as her tears fall. She is devastated. I hate seeing her so sad. With a dry mouth, I pat her shoulder.

At Mom's insistence, Dad comes home that night to tell us himself. He sits with his recliner in the upright position while

Mom and Brandon and I huddle on the couch. I sit on my hands to keep them steady, ignoring my own pain and hurt. My focus is on Mom.

"Brandon and Steph," Dad begins, "I'm moving out. Your mom and I want different things. I think this move is the best solution right now." He looks across the room, but not at us. He has never been one to share intimate emotions. I've never had trouble knowing when he is angry or disappointed or proud of me, but today I don't know what he's thinking.

Mom's tears look like a dam has broken inside her. I notice tears running down Brandon's face, too, but I feel unmoved. Dad's words don't reach me; I hear only the beating of my heart. I burn with anger at Dad for hurting them this way. *I'm tough, I can handle it. But they can't.*

The room feels small. I want to jump off the couch and rewind this one-sided discussion. Doesn't he remember that Brandon and I are his children? Doesn't that matter anymore? We aren't the cute little children that we were when he and Mom got married. We're teenagers now. *But we still need you.*

Still, I've been expecting him to leave. How have Mom and Brandon missed it? I'm angry with them for being so blind. Maybe the burden of reality was too much for them while I've been hunched over by the weight of it. Dad's heart hasn't been with us for some time. Damn him.

# CHAPTER 19

I stare at my white computer screen as I wait for Brooke's face to appear. My heart feels dull today. I rake my hand through my curls and sigh. It's September 2020. Michael has been in Hawaii for two months now and loving every minute. But even his happiness isn't enough to lift my spirits today. People continue to be careless in the United States with superspreader events. When will this virus end?

"Hey, Stephanie." Brooke's smile fills part of my screen. "How are you?"

"I'm feeling frustrated," I say. "People seem to be ignoring what Dr. Fauci and other experts are saying we should do. I'm enjoying my time at home and being able to write more freely, but I'm beginning to see this virus as a long-term problem."

Brooke nods in understanding. "What does that mean for you, Steph?"

"Well, I can't hug my husband, sit next to him, or touch him."

"What are you doing for your sensual needs?"

I raise my eyebrows. Brooke has been my therapist for over ten years. I realize nothing is not on the table in our discussions.

"I'm not doing anything."

"Okay," Brooke says, "I want you to wrap your arms around yourself. Your body can't tell the difference between who is doing the hugging, and stress-reducing hormones get released."

My arms reach around my shoulders, and I immediately feel my heart soften. I ignore my thoughts: *You look silly* and *you are so unlovable you have to hug yourself.* Words from my past creep in sometimes when I feel vulnerable. Those thoughts don't take the front seat anymore, but they spring to mind in these moments. The wounds always want to be the center of attention.

"Thank you, Brooke," I say. "I've never thought to do that. There were times when I was younger that I hugged myself, but it was automatic and private."

I take a deep breath and smile at her. Even though I find myself not being able to breathe sometimes from panic, I'm learning to catch myself and slow down.

"How are you doing staying at home?" Brooke asks.

"I'm doing well. I don't miss running around everywhere. I miss playing pickleball, but my concern over getting the virus is bigger than my need to play. Now that I'm not playing, my body is not in as much pain. I'm not needing regular massages or acupuncture. Something's going on with my right ankle. I have an appointment with an orthopedic surgeon in November. But the rest of my body feels pretty good."

We look at each other. The quiet pause in our conversation doesn't need to be filled. I feel seen and heard by her. There is so much value in this long-term relationship.

"I'm glad to hear you're doing well staying at home and that you're listening to your body."

"Me too. Do you remember the time I came in and was so exhausted from all the plates I was juggling? You suggested I lie down. I did and you covered me with a blanket. I did therapy with my eyes closed. I was so tired."

"I do remember."

We talk some more and then she asks if I'm enjoying being by myself so much.

"I am. Friends would say I am a flat-out extrovert. But you know, I believe I'm more introverted. I think I've been hustling for love for years and remaining loyal to others beyond what's healthy for me. Before Mike came into my life, I allowed myself to be treated as an expendable person. His love for me shifted my own love for myself. Perhaps when Covid is gone I will continue to hold on to a more introverted lifestyle."

Brooke leans forward in her chair—a sign our time is up.

"By the way," I say, "I saw a nurse practitioner about my enuresis. My urine was negative for any infection. It must be more psychological in nature."

"I'm glad you ruled out that possibility."

I twirl in my chair after we disconnect. My heart feels awakened. I hug myself in the quiet of my room. Dusty and Rascal sleep back-to-back on my bed. I let out a deep breath.

I'm over halfway through the first draft of my memoir. I sit at my computer, turn on Pandora, and punch away at the keys. The sense of freedom is sometimes overwhelming—as is the pain of digging up memories that still haunt me today. With a bowed head and hands in a praying position, I thank God for all that has been given me. I'm a witness to His/Her mercy. *Thank You for Your unending love.*

# CHAPTER 20

It's 1977 and I'm fifteen. No more guessing when Dad will be home. His clothes and essence are gone. Mom's bedroom door remains closed. When I put my ear to her door, I hear her crying and my stomach twists in knots. I don't know what to do for her. From my room, I listen to her muffled footsteps on their way to the kitchen to refill her drink and then a swish as her robe passes my door.

Dinner smells have disappeared. For some reason, this development bothers my brother. During one of Mom's appearances, Brandon corners her.

"Mom, it isn't fair that you don't cook anymore. I have had home-cooked meals until now, and I'm seventeen. Steph's just fifteen."

"It's okay, Mom," I say. "I'm fine."

I'm stunned by his reaction, by his concern for my needs, since I have always felt invisible to him.

The days pass and I ride my motorcycle or bicycle as much as possible.

"Hey, Steph," a friend from high school says over the phone one day. "Wanna meet a couple of us in the new neighborhood on Standifer Gap Road? We're gonna smoke some pot."

"Okay. What time?"

I feel like a fishing bob waiting to be pulled under. Maybe I'm already underwater. No one seems to be watching me anymore.

I find my friends and a few strangers sitting on the curb of an empty dead-end street. I release my hair from my helmet and join them. A woody, earthy smell mixed with fire floats around us as we take turns passing the pipe. I'm not committed to toking, but community in any form helps me move through the emptiness at home. Our house feels like a motel with each of us its separate occupants.

I shrink into myself. *So, this is how it goes. Your parents divorce and let go of you in the process.* I'd rather be playing ping-pong with Dad in our garage and being called to dinner by Mom than hiding out. I don't seem to care about much anymore except for sports. Now I'm sneaking off to smoke pot. Does anyone care about me?

Back home, I pull a brush through my hair and look into the mirror. *Who are you?*

Later, I head out for a babysitting job. I climb on my motorcycle, crank the engine, and rumble down our driveway. My body slouches as the wind rushes through my hair. The smell of cut grass and cow manure fill my helmet as I ride past a farm. I sneeze and try to get my hand inside the helmet to wipe my face. Within minutes, I arrive at my babysitting job.

"Hey, Steph," Bozo says. "Thanks for coming."

Bozo is the dad. I nicknamed him years ago when he and his other family lived next door to us because he reminded me of a clown. When I was twelve, I babysat his children—as long as my mom was home. Bozo spent time playing chess with me. I would carry my white chessboard with its pink and green plastic chess pieces to his garage. One day I noticed his jacket. A green patch was stitched into the jacket over the chest. The sleeves were torn and jagged.

"I love your jacket. *Hell on Wheels*. What's that?"

"I was in the army and that was our nickname." Smiling, he handed me the jacket.

"Really? That would be so cool to wear." His warmth lingered as I put it on over my shirt. "Wow, thank you."

I look at him now. He has gray hairs peeking through his mustache.

"I want to introduce my wife, Margaret, and her two children," he says.

The boys' names are Sammy and Calvin. We sit around their small den and tell stories for about thirty minutes. Bozo and I laugh when he tells them about the time he beat me at chess and I sent the lightweight board and chess pieces flying. I refused to play against him after that.

Margaret laughs with us before turning to her sons. "You two be good for Stephanie."

"We will," the boys chime back.

"I'm almost eight," says Sammy.

"And I'm eleven," says Calvin.

I become their regular sitter. Sometimes Bozo's children from his first marriage join us. When Bozo and Margaret return from their date, he pays me and I tuck away the money in my plastic-squeeze money holder.

Before Dad left us, he and Mom had told me my motorcycle days were coming to an end. They explained I would have to buy a car and sell the bike. I want to steal off with the motorcycle, so I don't have to sell it. I love my bike.

One day, Dad calls. "Steph, I think I found the perfect car for you."

"I don't want a car."

"We've been through this. You're not riding your motorcycle to school."

"I could change clothes at school."

"Do you want to see the car or not?"

"Fine."

Anger slides into my secret heart space. I cry for the loss of the wild freedom my bike has brought me.

The small used car lot is on the main drag in East Ridge. Dad stands on the gravel next to the multicolored banners waving in the wind. His hand covers his eyes from the sun as he looks for Mom and me. I wish I felt joy at seeing him and buying a car, but all I feel is loss. He opens my door and points me toward the lot. I hear the door close and Mom driving away.

"I think you'll like what I found," Dad says. "And it's in your budget."

The gravel crackles under our feet as we walk toward a small blue car. Another man comes out of nowhere and joins us. I barely listen as he tells us all the features of the car. Not wanting to disappoint Dad, I try to plaster a smile on my face.

"Wanna take her for a spin?" asks the salesman.

Dad looks at me. "Did you bring your driver's license?"

"Yes, sir."

Dad slides into the passenger seat while I adjust the mirrors. I look over and see that the car has a manual transmission.

"Dad, I don't know how to drive a stick shift."

"You know how to change gears. It's the same thing."

I ease out of the parking lot. To get to the main road, I must stop on a short, steep hill. I look in the rearview mirror and see another car behind me.

"Dad, make them move back. I don't want to roll into them."

"You can do this. Just give it some gas and slowly release the clutch."

I stall the car. "Please make them move." I feel pinpricks in my armpits. My wet hands grip the steering wheel. My heart races like the rpms in the car's engine.

"I'll show you a trick that you can use this once, but don't depend on it. Pull the hand brake up, give the car some gas, then release the clutch and brake at the same time."

Geez. He thinks I can do anything. Why won't he get out and make those people move back?

I do as he says, and we find ourselves on Ringgold Road. I didn't crash into the people behind me. Thank God. I manage a clean drive around East Ridge and drive us back to the dealership. My heart rate begins to slow down.

"We'll take it," Dad tells the salesman.

I drive away in my used Datsun B210, alone. I miss my dad already.

# CHAPTER 21

Andy's graduation from seminary looms. If I don't go, people will wonder why. Better to avoid questions and just go. On a warm June morning in 1978, I drive my blue Datsun up the mountain to Sewanee, Tennessee. The hour drive gives me time to reflect. It's been a while since I've seen him, since he isn't our Sunday school teacher anymore. His last year of school has kept him in Sewanee.

I decide I can always drive away if I don't like how things are going. But will I? Surely this day will be busy and focused on Andy and his graduation.

His face lights up as I cross the lawn and find him standing among the other students from the school of theology. "You made it," he says.

I cringe inside and smile. I'd rather be anywhere else than here.

"Why don't you stay with me until we gather inside."

"Sure."

I feel like a sardine crammed in its tin. I am the only non-student in the mass of black robes. The sun beats down on us as we stand outside the chapel's right transept. A breeze catches us from across the other side's open doors. I don't know how the graduates aren't melting. The robes sway as the students rock from side to side, moving to the organ music booming from inside the chapel. I curl my toes and straighten them. I hop from foot to foot. When will it be their turn to enter so I can sit down?

An hour or so later, I find a seat Maureen saved for me. Pomp and circumstance fill the chapel. The graduates process down the aisle. The pipe organ belts out hymns. Strong, jubilant voices join the music as goose bumps pop up on my arm. I realize my mouth is hanging open, gaping at all the fine details of the service. We congregants beat our handheld fans to push back the heat. After the long ceremony, the graduates recess out of the chapel, followed by the attendees looking for their loved ones.

"What did you think of the ceremony?" asks Andy.

I look at Maureen. I am not sure whom he's asking. She doesn't say anything.

"It was great," I answer. "So formal and *long*."

Andy smiles while sweat drips from his face. He stops someone and hands them his camera. "Would you take a picture for me?"

Andy stands between Maureen and me. He squeezes my waist and I laugh as I pull away from him. Click.

"We're going to join Joe and his family for lunch," Andy says. "We're parked over there. Follow us."

*Thank God. We won't be alone.*

In a crowd, I can rejoice with Andy and his achievements. Watching friends slap him on the back as we walk across the grounds to our cars makes me question my perceptions. He's so well-liked. Is he as bad as I think he is? Why does he want me? I love his attention and affection when it's just hugs and cheering me on. But he's gone too far.

After lunch, I pick up my purse and stand to leave. Andy stands too and gives me a back-breaking hug and thanks me for coming. I wave at the others and hug Maureen without much feeling.

I slip into my car and drive down the mountain. My thoughts are scrambled as I try to make sense of my relationship with Andy. I let out the breath I've been holding and crank up the radio. I want to hush my thoughts. He has a wife, yet he wants me in a sexual way. I'm young and dealing with my parents' divorce. Why can't he just help me through this difficult time? I feel anger creeping up to the surface more and more. I wish I could talk with someone.

All summer I agonize about my strange relationship with Andy. In bed at night, I stare at the ceiling with my thoughts running crisscross over each other. Does he love me? Is he using me? Where will our relationship go? He's married. I'm a teenager. He'll be moving back to Mississippi soon. I live here. I feel safe when I am in his arms—until he goes too far. Even then, my body responds. Why does this happen? What does it mean? What attracts people to do these things to me? What *allows* them to do these things to me?

Once again, softball helps divert my swirling thoughts. I throw every part of myself into every pitch and at bat. My success as a catcher continues to grow. People come to me after games and comment on my throwing arm and my fierceness behind the plate. I'm not sure what to do with these compliments. I smile and say thank you, but let the words bounce off me.

I also become bolder in protecting my pitchers from an opposing player's parent or from their own relative who yells at them behind the backstop. I even stop a game by facing one down.

At that game, an opposing player's dad stands behind the fence at my back and makes sounds every time my pitcher throws a ball to the batter. After a few minutes, I've had enough. His sounds are getting to my pitcher and me. The pitcher, Cathy, starts throwing balls. She's frowning.

"Ignore him," I say. "He knows how good of a pitcher you are."

She walks the batter.

"There you go, pitcher," he says, and laughs.

"Come on, Cathy. You've got this."

The heckling continues. "Hey, pitcher, pitcher. That's it, throw another ball."

I fling off my mask and charge at the man, the fence our only barrier. "What are you doing? You're an adult and she's a kid. Stop!"

I wish the umpire or some of the other parents would say something. I seem to be the only one who's willing to stand up to this man.

He continues with the noises. "Ehhh. It's not my fault she can't pitch."

I lose it. "Shut up!"

The man smirks at me through the fence. I realize he has succeeded at his game, so I kick dirt at him. One of my coaches hurries over to talk with the ump, who then tells the guy he must sit in the stands or leave. *I hope he rots in hell.* My body feels tense as my anger boils over. I'm sick of adults acting like children. Grow up!

There are no more incidents the rest of the season.

School begins in a few weeks. I will be in my junior year of high school.

We are in Mom's car heading to my great-grandmother's. Mom wants to take her to the grocery store since she never learned to drive, but she's eighty-five and manages to take care of herself. I adore this special woman but I haven't seen her in a while, so I join Mom. Great-grandmother took care of

Brandon and me for many years when Mom was single, before she married Dad.

As we turn onto her road, we see her pushing a grocery buggy near her driveway. Mom pulls in beside her and gets out, hands on her hips.

"Mama," she says. "What are you doing? We were on our way to pick you up."

"Hey, Patricia," she says. "Hey, Steph."

"Hi, Great-grandmother."

I get out and hug her. I try not to laugh at my mom. She's not happy that her grandmother beat her to get groceries, but I marvel at her spunk. Not being able to drive doesn't limit her activities. But I also admire how Mom loves her and tries to help her. It would be cool if I could take parts of them and incorporate them into myself.

"Mama," my mom says, "I told you I was coming to take you to the grocery store. Why did you walk and not wait for me?"

"I felt like getting out today. And they don't mind if I take one of their buggies. The people at the store know I'll bring it back."

Mom shakes her head. "Well, let us help you put them away. But first I need to pull the car into the driveway."

Great-grandmother pushes past us and waits for us at the bottom of her stairs.

I get out of the car and begin carrying the few bags inside. I love this strong, independent woman. I remember one time we came to pick her up and a truck was delivering a mattress. Mom went ballistic. Great-grandmother foils Mom's plans on a regular basis, but Mom gets along better with her grandmother than she does her mother. I move around the small kitchen and take a deep breath. I love the scents of burned bacon and her homemade apple-butter jelly. I'm glad I came with Mom today.

Later, back in the car, Mom says, "Mama is a mess. She knew I was coming over to take her to the store."

"I know, Mom, but she likes her independence."

Mom stops at the red light and changes topics. "Have you heard from Andy lately? How's Maureen's pregnancy going?"

"I think they're doing well. He's looking forward to moving back to Mississippi."

Mom merges onto the highway. "I know you'll miss him."

"Yeah, but I'm busy with school and friends."

"He's been so good to you."

*If only you knew.*

# CHAPTER 22

"Today, Ruth Bader Ginsburg has died at the age of 87," the TV news reports.

Something in me dies too. It's mid-September 2020. Mike looks at me from the other couch, mask on. "Now what?" his eyes say.

Covid deaths have climbed to 250,000. Protests for Black Lives Matter have ramped up as more and more Black people are being shot by the police. And now Justice Ginsburg is gone, leaving a large hole on the Supreme Court.

I take a deep breath and reach for gratitude. "She stayed alive as long as she could," I say. "It is time for her to rest. We must continue RBG's work. The torch has been passed."

Mike nods his head.

Over the past few years, Mike and I have attended peaceful protests in town and in Atlanta. I've become more active and political on his coattails. I wouldn't go without him.

Mike and a small group of people are working to revive the local Democratic Party in our rural town. In fact, he is their new president.

During a commercial, Mike stands, picks up our plates, and goes to the kitchen. The smell of balsamic and herbs follow in his wake. Dusty, our blind dog, stirs next to me as if he can feel the weight of RBG's death and our coming to terms with this reality. I get up and go to Mike. We touch our backs together and rub each other in a faux hug. My arms ache to hold and be held by him.

"We're going to get through this," he says. "We are."

"One day at a time."

Mike looks at me. "Al-Anon slogans are so applicable."

"Yes, they are. I'm glad for the years when I was a regular attendee."

"Me too."

Both of us have people in our lives who are problem drinkers.

As I load the dishwasher, I watch the birds eat their dinner in the many bird feeders in our backyard. I lift another prayer for the amazing Justice Ginsburg and for all those who have died of Covid-19. I know it will all pass, but when?

The political climate is toxic. The air we breathe may be toxic. Thank goodness for Sundays. Video church resuscitates me once again for another week of bleak news. May some fairy dust from RBG fall our way.

# CHAPTER 23

It's 1978 and I'm sixteen. As a high school junior, classes, sports, and friends fill my time.

Attending weekend parties becomes another activity. A student teacher not much older than we are invites some of us to her apartment one Friday night. She assists the coach for our basketball team. "I'll provide the alcohol," she says.

The five of us grin and nod our heads, saying yes to her invitation. Each of us drives separately to her apartment in a complex that sits up on a hill overlooking downtown Chattanooga. Lights twinkle in the cool night. I knock on her door and it opens right away. I walk in and am given an alcoholic drink. I smile.

We sit on mismatched furniture and talk and laugh. After drinking several bottles of Pink Champale, I'm on my knees with my face in the toilet bowl. Someone holds my hair back as I empty my stomach. I rinse my mouth and turn on the bathroom fan as I leave. The smell follows me out the door. My feet drag across the thick carpet as I find my keys. The temporary feeling of adulthood evaporates as my head spins. I want to go home. Debbie and Mary follow me out.

I stumble inside a public restroom downstairs, and my friends follow me in. We talk through the three stalls. My ears throb. Mary and Debbie finish first and sit with their backs resting against the bathroom wall. I can see their feet from the stall.

"Dad would be mad if he knew what I was up to," Debbie says.

"Yeah, so would mine," Mary answers. "Sometimes I wish he wouldn't keep an eye on me all the time."

I fly out of the stall. "You have no idea what it's like to not have a dad!" I shout while washing my hands. "You are so lucky."

Tonight, I can't hold in my anger. As I stumble past them, they reach for me. "Steph, come back," Mary says.

Once outside, I topple to the ground. Every time I try to get up, I find myself lying face down on the ground. Grass sticks to my face as I crawl to my car. I pull myself up and climb inside. The steering wheel feels cold. Anger fuels my body as I pull onto the highway.

I have an eighteen-mile drive to my house. Music blares inside my small car as I rant and yell. As I leave the main highway at the Shallowford Road exit and approach a four-way stop, I decide to try an experiment. I wonder how fast I can go and what gear I will be in when I drive through the intersection. It turns out I'm only in second gear when I run the stop sign.

I pass a darkened convenience store and see blue lights flash behind me. I laugh. This conversation should be fun. I bet I can fool the policeman. I pull over, roll down my window, reach into my purse, and pull out my license.

"How are you doing tonight?" the officer asks.

"I'm fine."

"May I see your license?"

"Sure."

He walks away with the license. I blow on my hands and squirm in my seat. He comes back a few minutes later.

"May I ask why you went through the intersection without stopping?" he says. His breath shows in the cold.

"I forgot it was there." I feel smug. This exchange is going well—except I hate to lie.

"Where have you been?"

"At a friend's house."

"Where are you going?"

"Home. I don't live far from here."

"Okay, I'm going to give you a verbal warning."

It takes all I have not to laugh. *A verbal warning?* I feel my body shaking.

"And I'll follow you home."

"Okay."

I continue home with the policeman staying behind me and the blue lights turned off. He drives away as I pull into the driveway. I deflate like a balloon once I get out of my car and a sense of sadness washes over me. Mom's bedroom lights are off. I stumble into the house and crawl into bed. My heart is heavy as I cover my head with a blanket.

A week later, Andy calls. "Hey, Steph. Maureen, Mark, and I are settled in back home."

"That's great," I say. "How's Mark?"

My response is so automatic. Act like everything is normal.

"He's doing all right. Gaining weight. The pediatrician here is taking good care of him. My ordination to the priesthood is next month. I want you to come. I'll cover your flight to Mississippi."

Damn. I try to brush him off but know I'll have to go. Everyone will expect me to. "I'll check with Mom," I say.

"Okay," he says. "Let me know as soon as possible. We have so much going on. I hope you can come. Talk to you later. Bye."

I'm glad he didn't have time to talk more. I hang up, lean against the kitchen wall, and close my eyes. My hands clench at my sides. I butt my head against the wall. Shit. Shit. Shit. I wish Andy would disappear and then I could forget about him.

Later that night, I tell Mom about Andy's call.

"That's fine with me," she says. "I know having you there will be special for him. You two are so close."

*If you only knew.*

Once again, I feel powerless. I don't want to go. I feel like a pawn being slid across the chessboard. My presence is required, and I don't get a vote. People at church would be surprised if I missed this special event. Andy would be hurt. I'm not as bothered by him since he moved back home; physical distance from him is just what I needed. When Mom asks me if I'm looking forward to going, I think *no, it will be awful,* but I keep these thoughts in my secret heart space.

A few weeks later, I board a plane and fly to Mississippi for Andy's ordination, which will be held at his home church. On the flight, I look at the clouds below me and wonder if I'll find the answers in them. What will I do if he makes a move on me? But he won't do that with all his family and close friends around. He's so close to his end goal of being a priest. Surely, he won't risk it.

A friend of his meets me at the gate. "Hi, you must be Stephanie," he says.

"Yes, that's me."

"Andy was tied up with visitors and asked me to pick you up. He's told me so much about you. I hear you play fast-pitch and basketball."

My hands play with the zipper on my jacket. My mouth goes dry. What else does he know? "I do. Do you like sports?"

"I'm not very athletic, but I enjoy sports."

He puts my luggage in his car and drives me to where Andy and his family are. I meet his parents and stay in their home. I feel weird all over. What would happen if they knew what he's done to me? Shame walks all over me. I would die if anyone knew. But I can't help fantasizing about asking them, "Do you know who your son is?"

Pretending that I'm excited to be here helps me move through the events leading up to the ceremony—anything I can do to deflect attention from me. The less I'm noticed the less I have to lie. My face reads like an open book. It's exhausting, but this acting is only for a few days. Everyone treats him like he's so special. *Is he a hero to them like he once was to me?*

For the ceremony, the church is decked out in splendor. I see some of his friends from Sewanee. They stand in the back in their robes, talking. Andy grins as he waits for the opening hymn. He catches my eye and winks.

Ugh. What is that supposed to mean? I'm grateful there are so many people here so I can slip through and around them and minimize contact with Andy.

The organ begins with loud trumpet sounds. Priests follow the cross as they swish by us in the procession. I know the service will be long. I can't wait to go home.

That night, friends of Andy's flow through his parents' home. Chicken wings, crackers, cheese, and fruit are plucked off the kitchen table. Laughter and conversation surround me. Andy is kept busy. I keep my distance.

The next day, Andy drives me to the airport. "I'm so glad you came . . . I'm grateful for everyone who made it."

I smile.

"Did you have fun? I know I wasn't able to visit much with you."

"Yes. I talked with your friends."

He watches the road and smiles. I look out the window, willing him to stay away from me. He hasn't even tried to hold my hand. I take a deep breath.

When we get to the airport, my legs want to run to the gate. He gives me a quick hug and peck on my cheek and follows me out of the car. I grab my suitcase and head inside. Maybe now our secret relationship has come to an end.

My seat on the plane is next to a window. I click the belt and take another deep breath as the passengers finish boarding. This trip should be my last obligatory event for a while. Thank God. I don't want to be forced into anything else. Airborne, I look at the clouds and think, *Maybe I won't see Andy for a long time.*

# CHAPTER 24

It's 1978. I have a new teacher for economics. His brown eyes do a quick scan of the small classroom, which is away from the regular classes and next to the basketball courts and locker rooms. I doubt that matters to him since he is new to CPS, but it's weird for me to be in a windowless room. Mr. Finnegan is short and muscular and cute. His jaw is square. He doesn't look much older than we are.

"My name is Gary Finnegan," he says. "I went to high school here some years ago and then I graduated from the University of the South with an economics degree." He smiles.

*Oh my gosh, he has dimples.*

Most of us lean forward in our desks. This teacher is much more interesting than economics.

"Will you be coaching football?" asks one of the players.

"I hope so. I'll definitely be the wrestling coach. I wrestled when I was a student here and at Sewanee."

Some of the wrestlers nod and smile.

Mr. Finnegan begins to teach, exuding authority. He needs to since he looks too much like one of us. I wonder how old he is. I'm sixteen and he looks like he's in his early twenties.

I can't take my eyes off him. He paces the room as he goes through the lesson he's prepared. *I wonder if he's shy, nervous.*

Several weeks into the semester, Mr. Finnegan, wearing a pale yellow pair of slacks, enters the classroom with a stern face. I cover my mouth with my hand. Other classmates have picked up on the same thing: his pants are so light we can see his boxer shorts.

Stifled snickers break through until we can't contain ourselves. Mr. Finnegan stops in the middle of the classroom and looks at us. "What's going on?" he asks.

Our heads swivel this way and that as we try to discern who will tell him—all the while laughing.

"Uh, sir," says Brian, one of our offensive linemen. "Your pants. We can see through them."

He looks down and presses his pants to himself. At first, his face turns red. We hold our breaths. Then he looks back up at us and his face melts into a smile.

*There go his dimples.*

"I guess I won't be wearing these again."

We dissolve into more laughter. My heart hammers as I wipe tears from my face. So Mr. Finnegan is humble too. Nice.

Our volleyball coach, Coach Williams, doesn't take himself seriously either. He's the one who calls me Fish. I wink at one of my friends and smile. As I take a deep breath, I realize I feel safe and happy. I'm not struggling with trust. Being in a full classroom and on a sports team keeps past fears away. I'm never alone.

Volleyball season starts the next week. The first day of practice, I get dressed in the locker room and pull up my knee pads. I wonder why guys don't play volleyball. Maybe the same reason girls don't play soccer? I join the others in the gym.

"Hustle up, girls," Coach Williams yells at us. "We're going to start off with my favorite drill." I reposition my knee pads as he points to the tall ladder. "We'll rotate who feeds me the ball."

Coach Williams climbs the ladder and throws balls at us. The white ball swerves through the air as it flies down at us. Sounds of grunts and knee pads sliding on the gym floor fill the gym as we return the balls to him. Some of us whisper to each other in between diving and retrieving.

"Hey, Coach," Karen says. "Whatcha doing on Halloween?"

"Not much. Handing out some candy."

We smile.

"Why?"

"Oh, nothing."

We make plans over the next few weeks for rolling Coach's house. A few days before Halloween, I pass him in the hall.

"Hey, Coach."

"Fish."

"Maybe you'll see us on Halloween night."

"Are you going to be trick-or-treating?"

"Not necessarily."

He shakes his head, rolls his eyes, and continues down the hall.

Coach Williams is so much fun to mess with. TPing his house is going to be great.

On Halloween night, Debbie drives her army green Jeep to his residence in nearby Harrison, Tennessee. She pulls straight into his short driveway with the headlights off. Giggling, we grab our white weapons and begin tossing them on top of the trees and into the backyard. We feel confident enough to sneak into the yard. I peek in their patio window where there is a break in the curtain. Coach and his wife are sitting on a couch, watching TV. I motion to the others to come look. The cold night air makes our chuckles look like we are smokers.

Coach Williams hears us.

"Run!" Debbie yells. We head for the Jeep.

Coach turns on the porch light and opens the front door. While we scramble into the Jeep, he yells something as he struggles with a garden hose. Laughter tinged with fear follows us down the driveway as Debbie backs out. I look up to see Coach's white undershirt chasing us down the driveway. Debbie shifts gears and we squeal in delight.

I'm so lucky to have great friends, fun coaches, and a cute teacher. Once more, I feel happy. And being at school gives me a break from being at home.

# CHAPTER 25

It's December 2020. I'm recovering from lateral ankle reconstruction. Even though my ankle surgery was only a few days ago, it seems that our family has been in crisis since October. First Dusty fell and broke his pelvis, then Joanna, my stepmother, was hospitalized for contracting Covid, and now my surgery. I don't even want to think *what's next*?

"Hey, Mom," Matthew says through my door. "Are you ready for breakfast?"

I smile as I look up at him. "Yes."

"I hope I made it the way you like it." He pushes through the door carrying a bowl of oatmeal, his mouth covered by a surgical mask.

I smell the mixed fruits he's added. His dark hair is disheveled from just waking up. When his puffy eyes glance at my leg, my heart melts at his care.

"Honey, it will be delicious because you made it for me."

I adjust the white undershirt of Mike's I'm wearing and slip on my mask. I pull myself up in the bed while keeping my leg elevated on a purple wedge.

Matthew hands me my bowl of goodness and returns to the kitchen. In a moment he comes back with a napkin and flax milk.

"Thank you, Matthew. I really appreciate your being here."

"You're welcome. How's your foot feel? Do you want me to ice it?"

I lean against the headboard. I've come a long way. I prefer being on the other side of caregiving but have learned to receive too.

Years ago, our church did a stewardship campaign on how we are enough in God's eyes. Pin-back buttons were passed around that said "I'm more than enough." I wore mine well past the campaign's end. Every time I put it on, my heart melted. I felt God's love through that simple button. I still have it.

In my earlier years, when I held on to my heart secrets, I was their hostage. No more. Working through my past grants me a window into myself and how my self-worth was wrapped up in other people's opinions of me. I felt like a leaking bottle trying to fill up. I recognize that I hustled for love. Now I check in with myself first, which is a huge shift. Loving who I am allows for me to receive love from others.

"Not too bad," I say to my son. "Ice would be great."

He pulls the door closed. I keep my room below sixty degrees at night because my asthmatic lungs like cold air. When I was young and tried to spend the night with friends, I would have to call my parents to pick me up because I couldn't breathe. One friend turned up the heat in her room and it felt like a sauna. I struggled to catch my breath and was scared, but she wouldn't turn it down.

Another time, a group of us were having a sleepover at my friend Catherine's house; she had cats. Pretty soon, I couldn't take a full breath. Trying to hide my struggle to breathe, I said, "Let's do something different and sleep in the back of your parents' station wagon."

In the car, my friends' breaths slowed down while I looked up at the stars through the back window. *Please help me breathe.* I laid still as long as I could, but I felt like I was in a casket being buried alive. Then my body took over and I bolted from the car, coughing and gasping for air. Catherine's parents were woken up. I called my parents to come get me. I was so embarrassed.

Matthew now returns with a cooler full of ice mixed with water. He lifts my cast and slips the wrap around my foot. As he elevates the container, I sense a tightness and a brush of coolness through the dressings. If care were an object, it would be the flow of cold water around my cast.

Matthew looks at me. "I know this is a silly question, but what was wrong with your ankle?"

"Not a silly question. It began hurting me on and off the pickleball court because I had laxity. The surgeon repaired some tendons and anchored them tighter to my bone."

After Matthew leaves to take a shower, I rub my legs. I hope he isn't too worried about me. Mike has been working and running all the errands; now he's running the house too. I know Mom, who lives three hours away, wishes she could be here to help me, but she needs to stay safe in her home. Talking on the phone with her every day keeps us close. Even though we don't talk about serious things, it's okay, because she lacks the capacity for that. She also knows I'm writing a memoir, but she doesn't ask about it.

I take a deep breath. Mike and Matthew are doing all they can to keep me from getting Covid. I focus on what I'm grateful for: Mike, our sons, Mom, our friends, our church, having Matthew's help, being able to have surgery, and so on. I know a Covid vaccine will be available soon, but how many more people will die before they can get their vaccination? Will the virus come through our home? All I can do for now is heal. That's my job. *Thank You, God, that I have people who love me and are here to take care of me. Please be with those who don't have anyone.* But even though I have Matthew here, and Mike when he gets home, I still feel lonely in the waiting.

On the other hand, being alone most of the time has opened my eyes to my need for quiet. I miss my friends and church and activities but am enjoying the time to myself. I'm aware I feel more like an introvert now. So strange. Perversely, Covid has afforded me this time to slow down and to write. The test will be when the virus has become a thing of the past and my ankle is healed. Will I make time to create a new way of living? Will I stay mindful of my needs or will I return to over-extending myself? Will I hold myself accountable to a balanced schedule? Will I ask for what I need?

I shift in bed. Somewhere I learned that staying busy equaled success. Important people are busy. As I hear the water rush through the pipes from Matthew's shower, I want to release my warped thinking into the flowing water above.

Later, Matthew returns to take my bowl and glass to the kitchen. This role reversal feels weird.

After he goes back to the kitchen, I hear him talk to the dogs as he takes them outside.

I sink back into my bed and close my eyes. Christmas is a week away, but my wrapped presents hide in my closet. I took the Scout motto to heart: *Be prepared.* I know that this year will be different, that the pandemic will keep our gathering to just the three of us. Michael will be in Hawaii, wearing a Hawaiian shirt and hanging out with friends. I push my hands together and send up prayers for Michael. *May he feel our love for him. May he feel love from his new friends. Please protect him. Amen.* I'll miss him, but I am happy that he loves where he is.

# CHAPTER 26

It's December 1978. Christmas break is around the corner. Part of me dreads it because Christmas hasn't been the same for us since Dad left. This year will be the second one without him. I'm going to miss school, my friends, and my church youth group. I stretch out on my bed and stare at the ceiling. Homework is light, so I think I'll play Jokari in the road. I grab my paddle, ball, and weight, and I'm met by Mom at my door.

"Hey, honey. I want to tell you something before you hear it from your grandparents. We're going to visit your birth father in Las Vegas. Your grandparents are coming too."

I stare at her. "Why?"

"We thought it would be good for you and Brandon to visit your dad."

"I'm not missing school."

"You're not going to miss any school. We're going after Christmas Day."

My palms feel sticky and my mouth dry. "That soon? What if I don't want to go?"

"You're going."

I push past her and jog downstairs and out the front door. My heart rate picks up. My body craves movement. I check for cars before putting the blue weight down that cradles the ball. An elastic string attaches the ball to the weight. I strap the wooden paddle around my wrist and whack the ball. I love how fast it comes back to me. *Whack!* Hitting a ball shuts out the pounding of my heart. I try to focus on the game.

But I'm going on a trip soon to see my birth father. My heart drops in my stomach, and walls are narrowing and trying to crush me. I snatch the ball and weight to move out of the way of an oncoming car. I wish we lived on a dead-end street.

I continue my game and realize it's been four years since I was forced to visit Don and Joanna in Sioux Falls. Brandon has made several trips to visit them, from Wenatchee, Washington, to El Centro, California. Don moves a lot but never close to the South, never close to us. Yet now I have to go visit him against my will.

A few weeks later, we board our plane bound for Las Vegas. We are crammed into seats across from each other, two on the side and three in the middle. My family ends up connecting with a gambler in the seat across from them. He's a big talker. I ignore them as much as I can, grab the *Delta Sky* magazine from the back of the seat in front of me, and try to read an article about high-rise buildings. Then I hear something about the stranger wanting to take us all out for dinner. Mom, especially, seems excited.

"That would be fun," she says.

"Then it's a deal," the man says. "How about tomorrow night?"

Over my dead body. Are they out of their minds? We don't know this guy. Why would he want to do that? Mom smiles at him. What is she doing? It's one thing that Mom and Dad are divorced, but bringing another man into this trip is too much. I feel like an emotional wreck. I don't want to be here and I think it's weird that my grandparents are coming with us.

Mom and Grandmother lean forward in the tiny airplane seats, listening to this guy go on and on. I turn my head in the opposite direction. The sky is light. I pull the miniature blanket across my shoulders. What a jerk. All he's talking about is himself, his money, and gambling. Disgusting.

I'm surprised to find myself mentally fighting for my parents. I thought I had released them as a couple. The anger I feel running through my body tells me another story. I still hold out hope that Mom and Dad will find their way back together. This jerk is interfering with that desire. I grip the armrest and try to ignore them.

Sometimes I don't understand myself. After my parents separated, I came home one day to find Mom leaning into Dad's arms against his car. I got out and slammed my door.

"You need to leave," I yelled. "You don't live here anymore and now you can't come back." Mom had just found her footing again and I didn't want him to mess it up.

Dad was taken aback. Now I wish I could have a do-over for that day.

I look across the seats and find that Brandon and my grandfather have joined the conversation. Great. I will not be a part of their plans. I will figure something else out. As the plane goes through its hard landing and reverse braking, I hold on tight to the armrests.

As soon as we walk into McCarran Airport, loud jangling sounds greet us. Chimes and beeps draw my eyes to the colorful lights of slot machines. At an airport? We march our way past them to baggage claim. The gambler joins us.

"Tomorrow night?" he asks.

The others nod their heads. I don't.

"That'll be great," my grandmother answers.

"You're staying at the Jockey Club?"

"Yes." She looks at Brandon and me. "Their father is putting us up there."

"I'll pick you up at seven o'clock."

*I'm not going.*

Don and Joanna meet us in their brown van outside at the curb. *He still looks ugly. He doesn't hold a candle to my dad.*

Don gets out of the van and greets Brandon and me with a hug. His cologne has a musty smell. I hate to admit to myself that I like it. I remember smelling it the first time we met. He hails a taxi for the others while Brandon and I climb into his brown van. I don't mind not riding with the traitors in the cab.

"Don and Joanna," I hear myself say, "may I spend the night with you tomorrow? The rest of the family has made plans to go out to dinner with someone they met on the plane. I don't want to join them."

Don's bearded face lights up in the rearview mirror. "Sure, Steph. You'll have to sleep on the couch. Our extra bedroom is a music room right now."

"That's fine with me."

We pull in front of the Jockey Club and greet the others.

"The Jockey Club isn't a casino," Don says. "It's more like a regular motel. I thought it'd be better than a casino for the kids."

"This is perfect, Don," says my grandmother.

"Yeah, this is great," Mom adds.

*I can't wait until I'm out of here.*

The Doobie Brothers' name fills the marquee across the street at The Hacienda. Colored lights flicker all around us. Don and Joanna walk us into the hotel. I feel like I'm in a dream. Las Vegas is a weird place. I take another glance at the casino across the street. I can't believe the Doobie Brothers are here.

Don picks me up the next afternoon in a two-door Chevrolet Impala convertible. The top is down.

"Are you hungry?" he asks.

"Yes," I answer.

Now that I'm in the car next to him, I don't know what to say. I wonder if he knows that he's the lesser of two evils. My hair blows in my eyes and I welcome the distraction.

"I want you to see some of the Strip," Don says, "but we'll eat at a neat little restaurant off it. The locals like this place. That's a sign it's especially good, but the food in Las Vegas is good in general."

I've never thought that much about food. I turn away from him and look around me. I feel my stomach begin to rumble. My hands are sweaty holding my hair, and I keep pulling on my scalp by accident. Car fumes rise from the Strip. The noise of the car heater and the wind and the overwhelming sights keep me off-balance. Why does he live here?

As Don whips the car into a parking lot, for a moment I feel like a movie star. The restaurant is the Dutch Pantry. I hope I find something I like. I thought we'd be having hamburgers and fries.

I don't want to upset Don. I wonder if he is working hard to get me to like him, because he seems excited to bring me here. Since I'm stuck with him, I need to get along and not make waves. He holds the car door open for me and the warm air wraps itself around me like a jacket. It's in the low 60s.

Compared to the buildings on the Strip, this place is small. Windmills decorate the sign out front. Inside, the place is filled with Dutch paraphernalia. Years ago, Grandmother gave me tiny Dutch wooden shoes after one of her trips to Holland. This place has that and more. A refrigerated case is filled with all kinds of cheese for sale.

As we are seated, my heartbeat is in another gear. I wipe my hands on my blue jeans and look around. We're given a menu by a woman dressed up in an apron and a sunbonnet.

My finger slides across the plastic covering the menu until I find a ham and cheese sandwich with fries. Yay. Something I can eat.

I tell Don what I'd like, and he places our order. Now what?

"Tell me about the sports you like to play," he says.

I relax and lower my shoulders as I talk. The meal passes before I realize it. When we're done, Don suggests picking some desserts to take home with us. "Joanna won't eat one," he says. "She's always trying to lose weight, but she looks great just the way she is."

I can't wait to see Joanna. I like her. She's fun, and her laughter is contagious. Brandon's earlier trips to visit them always included a story about Joanna and something silly she did. When I was forced to visit Don and Joanna in Sioux Falls several years ago, Joanna took me under her wing. I don't know what to expect now, but I know it must be better than going out to eat with that guy and my family.

As we drive, I breathe in the sights and smells of Las Vegas.

All of a sudden, Don says, "When are you going to start calling me Dad instead of Don?"

I feel my face heat up. I turn my head away from him. "I don't know," I mumble. I want to say *as soon as you act like one,* but I hold my tongue. Things are going okay between us. He is trying to be nice, so I'm willing to meet him halfway.

Ten minutes later, we pull into their driveway. Their house is so different from ours. Rocks and red tiles cover the roof. Their walls are made of white stucco, and an arch separates the driveway from the pool area. Joanna comes out to greet us. "Hello, Stepha-nee-nee," she says with a smile.

I laugh. "Hey, Joanna."

The next several days fly by. Michelle, Joanna's sixteen-year-old daughter, and I talk in her room at night. In Sioux Falls, Michelle and I slept in the same bed. She's shy and quiet. Don, an anesthesiologist, goes to work at different hours during the day. He's like a jack-in-the-box in the way he comes and goes.

My family comes for dinner one night. The meal lasts a long time. We sit in heavy chairs in the dining room. The orangish carpet is so thick and full, I have to pick up my chair to move it. Grandmother laughs more than I've ever seen her. I feel a weight inside of me as I watch these adults who have a history with each other.

We relocate to the open den. Grandmother makes herself right at home and takes off her shoes and lounges on one section of the couch where I sleep, with her mouth wide open in laughter. Don has a bar and keeps everyone's glasses filled. Is Grandmother drunk? She seems to be swooning in Don's presence. I've never seen her this way. Weird.

Michelle, her boyfriend Eddie, Brandon, and I return to the dining room and play board games. In a few days we will be going back home. I wonder if I'll miss being here. Our lives in Chattanooga are nothing like they are here. I'm fascinated by Las Vegas and Don's lifestyle. I wonder if I'll make a trip back by myself someday.

Don has been kind. I, too, have been nicer to him than when I was with him in Sioux Falls four years ago. I guess we're finally getting to know each other. Maybe this trip wasn't a complete waste.

# CHAPTER 27

It's now 1979 and school starts up again after Christmas break. I hurry to class and look up to see Mr. Finnegan coming down the hall as announcements echo around the building. My ears perk up at one announcement in particular.

"CPS will start offering fast-pitch softball this spring. Please see Coach Finnegan if you are interested in playing."

"Hey, Steph," he says. "As you just heard, CPS is going to start a fast-pitch program. Don't you play?"

"That's so cool. Yes, I do. So does Mary. We play on the Super Chargers in the summer."

"That's great. You can help me out." He laughs. "This will be a new experience for me."

"Of course, we can help. I can't wait to tell Mary. When does the season start?"

"Soon. I've got to recruit players and work up a practice schedule."

"Hmmm. I'll start asking around to see who else has some experience with ball." I skip past him on my way to class. My heart picks up the pace. *This is my sport. A place where I can shine. And Mr. Finnegan will be our coach . . .*

I slide into my desk next to Mary. "Did you hear the announcement about softball? Won't it be fun?"

"Yes," she answers.

The teacher calls our attention to the blackboard.

I whisper to Mary, "Mr. Finnegan's going to be our coach. He hasn't a clue on how to coach girls' softball. I told him we would help him."

She nods to me and looks straight ahead. I feel like grabbing a glove and calling a halt to class. I'm ready to start practice right now. Instead, I sit in my seat and try to tune in to our instructor.

Little by little, Mr. Finnegan pulls together a team. Since our small private school lacks a ball field, we'll practice at an elementary school. At our first practice, Mary and I look at each other and scowl. The grass on the field needs to be cut; rocks mixed with dirt make up the rest of it. At least there's a backstop.

"Mister—I mean—Coach Finnegan?" I say. "This field is a dangerous place to practice. The ball could jump off any of these rocks and hit someone."

"I hear you, Fish, I mean Yogi," he answers. I grin at the use of my softball nickname. I love seeing his dimples when he smiles. "I wish we had a better situation, but it's all we've got. I'll try to get here earlier next time and rake the infield. I won't hit any hard grounders."

I wonder if he knows how to hit a grounder. I guess we'll see what he's made of as much as he will learn about us.

"Okay, so Yogi, you're a catcher, and Mary, you're a center fielder?"

"Yes," we answer in unison.

"For everyone else, move into the positions where you feel comfortable."

The athletes shuffle around and mumble as they station themselves around the infield and outfield. No one comes to join me at the catcher's position.

Coach Finnegan's face frowns as he concentrates on placing the hits. Some balls ricochet from the loose rocks after they ping off the aluminum bat. He tosses the softball in his left hand and bats one-handed with his right. *Not bad.* He's no Barney or C.E., but I believe he'll do okay. None of the other athletes have competed at the level of fast-pitch that Mary and I have. Despite that, they are catching and throwing well enough.

Sweat pours down my face as I catch for our potential pitcher. Lori is the only one who went near the mound, so she's it for now. I reach into my mask with my fingers and pinch the drops from my eyes. I'm glad I brought my own catching equipment. It's much better than what the high school provided.

This season will be interesting. I love that I get to play more ball, and I feel my heart jump every time I see Coach Finnegan. He's so cute. His face seems to light up when he sees me too. One time, when I passed him in the hall, his head was down, and he was frowning.

"Hey, Coach," I said.

His head popped up and a big smile spread across his face. His cheeks seemed to turn a light red.

"Hey, Yogi."

*I think I'm falling in love with you, Coach Finnegan.*

At practices, we work well together. As the catcher, I take the throws home during infield practice and toss the balls to Coach Finnegan. We work in tandem shouting encouraging words to the players as they field the balls and make perfect throws to first base.

He leans into me in between hits. "I think we're going to do all right for our first year."

"I'm thinking the same thing."

I love that our small school might be able to put together a decent team with such limited resources. We aren't big or strong. We're definitely the underdogs, but we'll try our best against the more stacked public-school teams.

I put my hand in front of my face to shield my eyes from the sun. All of us are athletes who want to play ball. Our ragtag team may not take first place, but I don't believe we'll come in last either. I breathe in the smell of grass and dirt as I catch the ball from first base. *Thump.* I love the feel of the ball in my gloved hand. It's solid and predictable—two things I long for.

Several weeks later, we play our first game against Tyner High School. Mary and I know several of their players. A row of jiggling legs and nail-biting players sit on the bench as Coach Finnegan gives us last-minute tips. I feel my heart race as I squat behind the plate. When I play with my summer team, I know what to expect; we're all on the same level of intensity. I want my high school team to play well, but playing as a unit is more important to me. I draw energy from sports and my fellow players. I'm not getting this energy from home right now.

So much of my happiness takes place on the field with my friends. And now that I get to be with Coach Finnegan more, I want this experiment to go well. Sports fill a hole in me that sometimes feels a mile long. Softball is one game where I feel like a winner, and now I have *two* teams. And I'm good at it. I know that to my core. No one can take it from me.

At our first game, Lori, a senior and our only pitcher, does her best on the mound. The hitters on the other team have seen faster pitches and are making adjustments. They cross the plate twenty times while we score ten runs. After the game, we line up and tell the other players they played a good game. Then we huddle in the grass around Coach Finnegan.

"Not bad. Not bad, girls," he says. "This is our first time playing as a team, but ten runs aren't anything to sneeze at."

"Coach?" Lori raises her hand. "I need more practice on the mound. I'm sorry about all those hits."

"You did great," he responds. "We have areas to improve and will work on them at practice next week. We're going to get better."

We stand and put our hands in the middle of the circle and pray. Then we raise our hands in the air with a shout. I find Coach Finnegan's face under the raised hands. He winks at me. My heart melts as I smile back. I could look at his face all day.

# CHAPTER 28

It's February of 2021. *Ding-dong. Ding-dong.* My skin crawls as the doorbell echoes in the hallway. I hobble to the front door in a booted foot and hiking shoe. I hope I can handle her energy and nonstop talking today. My patience is wearing thin. Being cloistered as I am, any interactions feel invasive. Now that I am home all the time, I find that I like the quiet. I like being by myself.

I open the door to see the stout blonde woman, hair pulled back tight against her head. She pushes past me, armed with cleaning supplies. Her mask is made of thin polyester material. Deidra looks like a robber instead of a house cleaner.

"How're you today? How's your foot?"

I open my mouth to answer, but don't get the chance.

"Isn't it great you can walk now? I bet you're glad to be out of that cast. Six weeks must've seemed forever. Do you still need your knee roller and walker? I bet you can't wait to get out of that boot. Want me to start upstairs?"

I nod.

"Okay. How're your pups doing? I bet they are glad their mommy can walk again."

I want to flee from her presence. It's like she's the virus—something making its way from person to person and leaving behind discourse. I need my house cleaned because of my allergies, but I'm not sure it's worth having someone in my home. I'm the one who has called upon her services, yet I yearn for peace and quiet. Deidra moves and talks too fast for me. Instead, I nod again and turn toward my room.

I don't think I can take much more of her chatter. I'm not comfortable with the type of mask she's wearing either. Dr. Fauci says that type of mask isn't safe. Wearing two layers of material is better. *Thank God Lisa drove me to the health department last month. At least I have one dose of the Moderna vaccine.* Mike was one of the first to get a Pfizer vaccination in December 2020. After almost a year, Mike and I can wrap ourselves around each other again. When we first kissed on the lips, it felt like I could breathe again.

I hurry the pups into my bedroom. I don't mind their company. They're quiet, attentive, and ready for a nap. One at a time, I lift them to the bed. It's not all Deidra's fault that I feel this way. Being around anyone makes me uncomfortable. I'm enjoying my own company and Mike's. Being on Zoom for meetings and therapy don't threaten me either. I'm not sure I will keep Deidra for long.

I turn on my computer. I love disappearing in my writing and ache to write more of my memoir. It's as if I see a light shining in the distance. The more I write, the closer to it I get. I'm amazed at how returning to my past is helping me understand the little girl inside me. Writing allows me to step back and take a more objective look at myself and how I got to be where I am. I have an hour now before I'll need to elevate my foot. As I slip my right-footed boot under my desk, I take a deep breath and then hear footsteps heading downstairs. *Please don't bother me.* Deidra makes our large house feel tiny.

I have allowed so much busyness to keep me from taking a solid look into myself that I don't want anyone or anything to slow me down. Now that I am staring down my past, I don't want to be kept from it. I feel trapped by Deirdra's energy and inquisitiveness, but I need to keep digging.

I hear a light tapping on my bedroom door.

"Yes?"

Deidra pushes through my door, her mask below her nose.

"Hey. Do you want me to mop upstairs? I can't remember what you said last time."

"You don't have to do the upstairs every time. There isn't much traffic up there these days."

"Okay."

Her eyes glance at my computer and I want to cover the screen. She turns to look at the pups.

"Aren't they cute? I just love dogs. My neighbor has four or five. Sometimes they come and dig in our yard. My husband is talking about putting up a fence."

"Would you mind covering your nose?"

With a quick motion, Deidra lifts the mask higher. I feel like an adult dealing with a child. Why doesn't she wear her mask the right way? I don't want this virus. I'm proud of myself for speaking up for my needs. "Is there anything else?"

"So, no mopping upstairs today?"

"Right. Thank you."

As she leaves, a whiff of perfume hangs above me. All is quiet except for the pups' breaths behind me. My fingers reach for the smooth keyboard. Maybe I'll get a few words down before I'm interrupted again. We need our house cleaned while I'm out of commission. Mike is busy working and taking care of me and the house, but I don't know how much more I can take.

*Focus.* So many people have died from Covid. A sigh escapes my body. A woman is in my house that I don't want here but need. Am I letting my boundaries slip again? How did I end up hiring the wrong person? Out of the blue, I'm hit with a different reality: I'm afraid of her. I feel like I can't breathe when she's around—even though I can breathe. I don't feel safe with her in the house. *Lord, please don't let Deidra be a carrier.* She doesn't seem to respect Covid. I will let her go. I'd rather deal with allergies and asthma than the virus, and I don't want to feel afraid in my own home like I did with Mike at the beginning of the pandemic.

My cell phone rings. Mom asks me what I'm doing.

"I'm trying to write, but I'm having a hard time focusing. The new house cleaner is here. She isn't wearing the proper type of mask and has it below her nose. I've just realized I don't feel safe around her. And she won't stop talking. She's nice, but pushy. I like her cleaning suggestions and all, but she's getting under my skin."

"She sounds like a handful."

"Yeah. I don't know how long I can keep her. I'd hoped to have her until I can clean the house again myself. We'll see."

"It's awful how many people are dying."

"It's terrible. I sure hope everyone will get their vaccinations as soon as they're available. I feel a layer of safety from just having the first one. I'm so happy Mike and I can sit next to each other, and he doesn't have to wear a mask."

"Me too. Well, I won't keep you."

"I love you, Mom."

"I love you too."

I fill my lungs with air and let out a deep breath. I'm so glad we talk every day. I think of what Brooke, my therapist, would say about me and my cleaner. I hear her challenge me: *Are you taking care of yourself? Is she doing what you hired her to do or are you afraid to hurt her feelings and let her go?* I answer in my head, *as soon as I can walk* . . . or earlier.

The full inhalation calms me. No coughing or breathing problems right now. Staying inside and taking the right medicines affords me release. I was seeing my allergist, who makes sure my lungs are doing well, every four months. Now we are using teletherapy. I pull up a search engine and look up Covid deaths in the U.S. Close to five hundred thousand people have died so far, and it's only February. I push away from my desk, pluck the pups from the bed, and go to sit on the couch and elevate my foot. Deidra pops into the room.

"Oh, there you are. I'm going to clean your room while you're out here."

I close my eyes, hoping to make the numbers disappear—and hoping to end any further conversations.

# CHAPTER 29

It's the summer of 1979. I'm seventeen. My mom is chipper this morning. Then she drops a bombshell.

"We have all these empty bedrooms. I thought it would be nice to have more people living with us."

I know she's feeling better, but this much change can't be good.

"Really?"

"Yes. I've asked Ginger and her daughter, Moon, to move in with us. I thought summer would be a good time."

Huh? I really don't want extra people here, even though I love Ginger. She will be a blast. I don't know Moon as well. Such a strange name. None of my friends have other people living in their homes. They have their parents living with them.

"Well, it's your house," I say. "You can do whatever you want. I like Ginger a lot. She would be fun to have around."

I've known and loved Ginger, who has taught dancing with my dad at the Arthur Murray Dance Studio, for the past seven years. I used to ride to Florida with her and her boyfriend, Greg, when the dance studio went on cruises. Greg would drive us in his convertible in the caravan of cars.

Mom smiles. "I thought you'd be happy about it. She'll pay rent and that will help me too."

"When are they moving in?"

"Next weekend."

I feel weird that Ginger teaches dancing lessons with my dad. He should be living here, not Ginger. I guess he doesn't have a say in the matter, but still . . . I know he's dating someone, but I can't let go of wanting our family back together. I feel cheated that we've broken apart. Keeping busy with my friends and sports is good so I don't have time to feel sad, but sometimes that's not enough. I think I will love having Ginger here, but her presence won't make up for his absence.

Brandon is a volunteer fireman and goes to college. He spends the night at the fire station most of the time. It's good that he is gone so much because I'm not sure he'd like being here with a bunch of women.

The following weekend, Ginger moves into the guest bedroom downstairs, next to Brandon's room. Moon moves into the guest bedroom down the hall from my room. She is ten and Ginger must be thirty, ten years younger than my mom. It's like we have a commune here. I think about when my parents hung orange and green beads in our old house to separate the den from the hallway and burned incense. We walked to a nontraditional beat. I felt cool, albeit different.

A week later, Mom says, "Ginger and I want to go dancing on Friday night. Would you mind taking care of Moon?" I agree.

While they're out, Moon and I watch TV and eat Jiffy popcorn. I want her to have fun and not miss her mom.

"I like living here," Moon says to me. "Your mom is so nice."

"I'm glad you do. Yes, Mom is nice. She's very loving. It's cool having you and your mom living with us." I don't want to hurt her feelings, but it would be even more fun if Moon were closer to my age.

Mom and Ginger go out most every weekend, while I take on the role of big sister for Moon. She has lots of aunts and uncles, but they live on the other side of Chattanooga. Her brother lives in Memphis with their father. Ginger loves Moon but seems to need the same things as my mom. They both seem to crave freedom from responsibilities, even though Mom has always been the stable parent. Now, she's off having fun. I don't quite understand her need, but I'm happy she's having fun.

When they aren't out on the dance floors in downtown Chattanooga, they are home with us. In our den, we put the cassette player on the hearth and listen to KC and the Sunshine Band or Donna Summer. I help Mom and Ginger drag our heavy circular table out of the way to make room for a dance floor.

"Get down, get down" bounces off the walls. Ginger dances with me and we laugh. Mom and Moon boogie down too. I wish we could be this way more often. It feels like a party when all four of us are together. Mom has come back to life and I love seeing her smile. I watch her twirl on the carpet as I collapse on the couch, giggling. I hope this fun time lasts.

As the weeks go by, Ginger and Mom and their friends meet downtown for dancing and backgammon.

"We have so much fun," Mom tells me. "Ginger and I have found some dance partners. They're younger and they can dance well."

"How old are they?"

"In their early twenties or so. We aren't dating them, although they are handsome!"

I don't know what to think. I want her happy, but these guys are closer to *my* age. I feel like I'm the parent. I know Mom married when she was sixteen years old and I know that she's experiencing a sense of freedom she's never had. I want her to be my mother and have fun at the same time. I doubt my friends can relate, so I hold these thoughts close. Maybe I should let go of trying to be *normal.*

The next week, Mom's eyes sparkle when she asks if it would be okay to invite their dance partners over for dinner. "Would you mind, honey? I want you to meet Tim and Randy."

"No, that's fine."

Is she asking for my permission? My sense of responsibility is on high alert. Somebody needs to be in control. "Do you want me to cook dinner?" I ask. "Like spaghetti? Moon and I can serve you in the dining room."

"That would be great. Thank you. I know they're younger, but they're good guys. You'll like them."

Moon and I come up with a plan. We'll serve them as if they were at a nice restaurant. Moon is excited to help and we pretend it's a game. Both our moms act like teenage girls all week. The four of us dance and play backgammon in the evenings.

On Friday night, the doorbell rings. As Mom and Ginger greet the young men, Moon and I watch from the top of the stairs. We wear dark clothes, pretending we are waitresses. Both guys are close to my age, blond, muscular, and smelling of cologne. One of them carries a bottle of wine. What are Mom and Ginger doing with these young guys?

I notice one of them take a deep breath before introductions are made. I feel like laughing at the situation, but deep down I feel unmoored. This whole scene feels ridiculous. Is anyone in charge? Am *I* supposed to be?

"Hi, Stephanie. I'm Tim. Your mom talks a lot about you."

I'm sure he thinks of the fact that I'm closer to his age than my mother is. His handshake feels stiff and unsure. "It's nice to meet you."

Mom and Ginger give the men a tour of the house as Moon and I prepare the salads. I hear their laughter downstairs. How awkward and weird this situation is.

Moon and I wait on the diners. Mom's face is lit up and her hands are flying around while she talks. She is laughing at everything these twenty-year-olds say. Ginger is also smiling but not working as hard as Mom to impress them. When I look at Mom, I see a neediness in her—like she wants to turn back time. Her makeup looks softer on her face. Her body leans forward as if to absorb every morsel.

She and Ginger act younger while the youthful men try to act older. The men seem to sit up straighter while the women pour themselves out. It seems we are all pretending to be someone else tonight. I feel confused but willing to go along for the sake of my mom and her joy. But I'd rather it was Mom, Dad, Brandon, and me at the table, laughing and enjoying each other's company. I feel a hole in my stomach thinking about what I don't have.

When I meet Mom's eyes, I see gratefulness. My chest fills and I promise myself to do whatever I can to make her happy. She's been sad for so long. If helping her without judgment makes her happy, then I don't mind. If there was such a thing as a parent patrol that wanted to stop Mom's footloose living, I would object and defend her. Hearing her laughter eases my sadness. She and Ginger can dance all they want.

"Would anyone like more salad?" I ask. When they are ready for dinner, Moon and I return with their spaghetti.

# CHAPTER 30

I wake up, stretch, and feel hope. It's July of 1979. The sun is shining, Mom's happy and Ginger's son, Scott, is coming for a visit. We are the same age, but it's been a long time since I've seen him. Scott attended St. Stephen's part of the year with me in fifth grade. I go to the bathroom across the hall and look at myself in the mirror. My skin is darkened from the sun, and my brown eyes stare back in amusement. I squint and make faces. I stick my tongue out and smile at myself before returning to my room.

I finish making my bed and look around with fresh eyes. My red beanbag chair looks deflated in the corner. Above it, I have a bouncy, spindly mobile with colored balls on the ends. Probably looks kind of weird, but I like it. My green carpet is thick and even, but I still miss the psychedelic shag carpet at our old house. My bedspread is a colorful patchwork of designs. The rest of the furniture I've had since I was eight years old—Grandmother's provincial furniture. Sports trophies fill every available space. I smile as I think of the memories they hold.

As I head to the kitchen, Ginger's perfume lingers in the air, and I admit that I love having her here. Mom's idea is working out so far. It's fun having more people here.

Ginger's already gone downstairs with her breakfast. Instead, I find Moon in the kitchen pouring herself some cereal. She squinches her nose when I ask if she's excited to see her brother.

"Eh. Maybe."

Milk splatters on the counter. Moon, not a morning person, walks hunch-like over to the table and plops down. I heat two Pop-Tarts in the toaster, grab a plate and a glass of chocolate milk, and head to my room, where I nestle in my beanbag chair. Mom's insistence that we eat only in the kitchen doesn't seem to apply anymore. Part of me misses her rules and knowing what's expected of me. I wonder what else I can get away with, but I feel conflicted about it. I want to hold the line and be who Mom needs me to be, while another part of me wants to take advantage of her distraction. I decide to think about something else.

I wonder if this kind of lifestyle will be what dorm life is like when I go to college. I wipe a few crumbs from my mouth onto the plate, being careful not to get any on the carpet. Brandon won't be returning to school. He says he already knows everything because his school overprepared him for college. Instead, he's going to drive a tractor trailer for our grandfather's battery business. I wish he wouldn't drop out.

Mom received her GED through mail correspondence, Dad got his GED in the Navy, and Brandon went to college for one year. I will be the first in our family to graduate from college. Maybe I'll be a doctor. I'm not good at taking standardized tests, but I get good grades at school without trying hard.

I swallow the last of the chocolate milk and take my cup and plate to the dishwasher. From the living room windows, I watch Mom pull weeds. The lawnmower's sitting by the driveway. I wish I could help her, but allergies still keep me away from trees and grass. I'm not drawn to yard work like Mom, but

I would like to help her. She works so hard. Feeling sad about my limitations, I head to softball practice.

I make it home before Scott arrives. I shower and put on my blue jean cutoff shorts and a red top. I think the red looks good against my dark skin. I'm not interested in Scott as a boyfriend, but I want to make a good impression. Being liked means a lot to me. I hope he is good at playing ping-pong. It's hard to find anyone good enough to play me. I wonder what he thinks about his mom and sister living here.

Scott pulls in around 9:00 p.m. Ginger opens the door as Mom and Moon and I stand at the top of the stairs to welcome him. Moon walks down the stairs and gets a rough hug from him. He looks more handsome than the last time I saw him. Older too, like a mini man. This visit may be fun, I think, glad he'll be here for a little over a week. Maybe we can see a movie sometime.

We go about our normal activities while Scott visits his grandmother, uncles, aunts, and old friends. One night, Scott asks me if I'd like to go see a movie.

"Sure. I was going to suggest the same thing. When do you want to go?"

"Let's go tonight. I hear *Apocalypse Now* is showing at East Gate."

I'm not crazy about seeing this depressing-sounding movie, but it's nice to be asked out. Plus, Scott drives a cool car.

After Mom tells us to be careful like she always does when I go anywhere, we head out. Scott and I talk about our schools along the way. Soon, we're leaving the highway.

Scott idles the car in neutral at a red light. All of a sudden, he's trying to get the car into first gear and his eyes look frightened. I look out the side window, so I don't embarrass him, but just then, we are rammed from behind. Our car leaps forward into the intersection while Scott clamps on the brakes.

I smell engine fluids. Cars pull over. "Are you all right?" I ask Scott.

"My neck hurts. I braced myself. I'm glad you didn't know what was coming. That guy came at us fast." He gets out, but I stay put.

Soon, sirens make their way to us. The police talk with both drivers on the side of the road, but it's clear as to who's at fault. After thirty minutes of paperwork and discussion, we are allowed to leave, and Scott drives us home. The back of his car is smashed. I feel lucky that I don't have any physical pain and the car isn't mine.

Mom and Ginger come out to inspect the car and cluck over us. We eat leftovers and I go to bed early. As I lie down, I say my prayers.

*Thank You for protecting us tonight. I'm so glad I didn't tense up. I hope Scott will be all right. I love You. Our Father, who art in heaven, hallowed be Thy name. Thy kingdom come, Thy will be done, on earth as it is in heaven. Give us this day our daily bread and forgive us our trespasses as we forgive those who trespass against us. And lead us not into temptation but deliver us from evil. For Thine is the kingdom, the power, and the glory, now and forever. Amen.*

On the eve of his last night here, Scott suggests we stay home and watch the CBS late-night movie.

I pop popcorn and wait for Scott in the den. Mom, Ginger, and Moon are in bed early tonight. Scott enters the room wearing only white underwear. I turn the other way and giggle. What does he think he's doing? Is it okay for him to do this? He's not my brother. I guess I'll act cool about it. I hand him the popcorn and cover myself with a blanket. Maybe if I cover up, he'll do the same.

The Zenith TV sits at an angle to the couch. I keep my face to the left with Scott on my right while he crunches on the popcorn.

"I was hot, so I thought I'd just wear my underwear. I hope you don't mind."

"No. I've seen my brother in his underwear plenty of times."

The next thing I know, he has turned my face to his and kisses me. I'm not attracted to him, but I don't want to hurt his feelings and I figure a few kisses won't hurt. I don't know where this attention is coming from, though. We went out a few times after the accident, but that's it.

"Why don't we go to your room?" he asks.

Can't we watch the movie as planned? My heart rate takes off and my palms start to sweat. Why does everything with boys have to do with wanting more than just being together? I don't want anything to happen between Scott and me. I'm not interested in him. And, between Mom and the little education I've had, I'm afraid of sex and pregnancy. But I follow him to my room anyway.

I'm starting to wish Mom was still awake. I sit on my bed and Scott pushes me down so that I am reclining on my pillow. He begins to kiss my neck. What is he doing? He starts sucking my neck.

"Stop. I don't want a hickey."

It's as if I haven't said anything. He becomes more forceful, and I finally push him off of me. "I better not have a hickey. I start volleyball practice tomorrow."

Scott laughs and then lies on top of me and tries to reach into my panties. I feel his muscles tighten as he uses more force. I can feel his hardened penis.

"Get off me! If you don't, I'm going to scream!"

Scott rolls off, red-faced. I'm furious. I look in my vanity mirror and see a hickey on my neck. Now I feel used, but he leaves the room with a triumphant expression. I feel deflated and confused. Why did this awful thing happen to me? What did I do to encourage it? Is it my fault? Thank God, he didn't rape me. I think about what happened to me in second grade.

My emotions flip to rage. I hate him. I hope I never see him again. I want to hurt him like he did me. Why do guys only want to get in my pants? Damn him! Even my muscles weren't enough to fight him.

Scott leaves for Memphis the next day without a word. I, too, remain silent. I don't tell Mom or anyone else what happened. I'm not sure what to do with my emotions. I feel embarrassed and ashamed, and my gut feels hollow. If Mom and Ginger knew, it could mess up their friendship or, worse, the incident might be swept under the rug. My head spins with so many questions and feelings. I clench my fists, wishing it hadn't happened. Another secret to tuck away in my heart space. Will I ever find someone who treats me well and loves me for who I am and not what I have up my skirt?

# CHAPTER 31

I stare at my computer. I notice it's March 2021, but I'm back in my seventeenth year. Why did I stand up to Scott and not Andy? Is it just because we were the same age? If so, why did that matter? I shift in my chair. Scott used his physical strength against me. That was a first. And I didn't feel shame when the assault happened. Instead, I felt fury.

I'll ask Brooke her thoughts. Teletherapy is in half an hour.

I take the pups for a quick walk in the sunshine. As I drag them back toward the house, the birds seem to wish me well through their songs. Writing is allowing me to take a deeper look into the past. I'm amazed I can go back to these moments in time and relive them, but it's not easy work. I feel confident, though, that when I finish the memoir, I will be able to let go of the past. Writing is well worth the time and effort. Talking about it with Brooke further eases the pain of reminiscing, because I'm able to dissect the past with her. Each time I go there either through writing or teletherapy, the trauma becomes less heavy.

The dogs lap water from their bowl and I return to my office. When Brooke's face appears on the computer screen, I tell her I just finished writing something in the memoir that I want to talk with her about.

"Okay."

"Do you remember me telling you about the family who lived with us? The mother and her daughter, Moon? And how the mother's son, Scott, came for a visit and pushed himself on me?"

"Yes, I remember."

"Well, what hit me as I wrote about it is that I had used my voice. Why did I use it here but not with Andy? Or even with the seventeen-year-old when I was in elementary school? I don't understand the difference."

Brooke looks at me sympathetically. "Andy and the seventeen-year-old were in a position of authority. Scott was your age and your equal. He did not hold any authority over you."

I take a deep breath and look back at Brooke. I feel the truth hit me along with sadness.

As if reading my spirit, Brooke asks me what is going on right now. I take another deep breath.

"I wish I could have used my voice no matter who was taking advantage of me or how old they were. I wish I knew then what I know now. I can't help but wonder if I'm responsible for other girls Andy might have molested since me. In the beginning of our relationship, I told Mike about what happened to me when I was a child and as a teenager, but I have never tried to contact Andy's superiors. My focus has been on healing myself all these years. The #MeToo movement opened my eyes to the many other people who have been molested or worse. I've felt less alone since the movement began. And how did my seven-year-old friend find her voice when the seventeen-year-old tried to molest her? What did she have that I didn't?"

"You've been hard on yourself for a long time. I think what's most important is that you *have* found your voice. You *are* healing from the past. Writing is giving you a chance to further explore these experiences. You're giving yourself the gift of time."

I nod in agreement. "Do you remember me telling you about when I was in counseling with Sam, our former priest?"

"Remind me," Brooke says.

"He showed me that I did not have to keep friends out of a sense of loyalty. It had never entered my mind that you could stop being someone's friend—especially with someone whom everyone thought was great, like Andy. Sam encouraged me to write a letter to Andy, telling him that I needed to cut off our relationship. Mind you, I was in my early thirties. Heck, Andy was one of the priests who married me and Mike. How crazy is that? Anyway, I wrote the letter, and Sam mailed it for me. A week or so later, Sam received a phone call from Andy, who wanted Sam to give him my address and phone number.

"Sam told him no and ordered him not to call again. When Sam related this exchange to me, he wadded up a piece of paper and threw it in the trash can. 'That's what I think of him and his call,' he said. 'He won't be bothering you again.'

"It took writing that letter to begin the process of setting myself free from that relationship, and the thought of Andy trying to find me made me feel cold all over. When Sam tossed the paper away, though, I felt protected and seen. I feel the same level of care from you."

"Stephanie, it's an honor to work with you."

I smile at her and take a deep breath. "Guess what?"

She smiles at me and waits for my news.

"Mike and I have had both our vaccinations! We are back to kissing, hugging, and snuggling next to each other. Since he's wearing a mask and other protective gear at work, he doesn't need to wear one at home."

"That's great, Stephanie."

"I don't want the virus and will do whatever I need to to keep it away. At least I'm not as panicked anymore. The vaccinations and masks give me confidence. I trust the science and know wearing an N95 or KN95 mask works."

I feel lighter after our conversation and my body relaxes. I know I'm on the right track.

# CHAPTER 32

Curiosity brings me to church on a Wednesday at noon. It's late July of 1979. I enter the quiet nave and find a small group of fellow parishioners sitting in one of the transepts. Reverend Wilbanks is presiding over the ceremony—a healing service. The sun shines through the stained glass windows and colors the floor beside our chairs. A sense of peace and quiet surrounds me. The courtyard door is open, so I hear the gurgling from the fountain outside; the sound soothes my soul. The short, intimate service ends with each of us kneeling at the altar. When it's my turn, I feel the weight of the priest's hands on my head.

"Stephanie," he starts. "I lay my hands upon you in the name of our Lord and Savior, Jesus Christ. Beseeching Him to uphold you and fill you with His grace that you may know the healing power of His love. Amen."

"Amen," I respond.

The warmth stays with me as I get into my car. I'm reminded of God's love for me and I know I matter. I think about holding out my hands and picture God pouring an endless stream of life-giving water into them. I know I will attend this service throughout the rest of the summer. For just a second, I wonder how normal it is for me, a seventeen-year-old, to attend a weekly healing service. I push the thought away and decide I don't care.

Reverend Balch, my main priest since birth, is retiring. A new priest will start at the end of the month, which means change, something I don't like. The soon-to-be priest, Dr. Jim Curtis, had a big write-up in the religion section of the *Chattanooga Free Press*. I sit on my bed with the article spread out. He's married and has a six-year-old daughter. In the accompanying photo, he looks young. His smiling face looks back at me, but he isn't Rev. Balch. I feel like crying, but the tears won't come. I haven't been able to cry for some time now. Anger has too strong a grip on me. I wrap my arms around myself and hope the healing services can help me.

A few weeks later, I go to the Youngs' house for a youth group swimming party. Man, they have a nice house. I walk to the door and hear the others at the party in the back. I can't wait to swim with my friends.

After Mrs. Young greets me, I pull aside the sliding glass door. The pool is blue and inviting. Our youth group fills up most of the space. I undress to my bathing suit and jump in. I love my church friends. We all go to different schools, so being together on Sundays makes our time special.

We're treading water in the deep end when we notice a gathering of adults just inside the sliding glass door. "I think the new priest is here," someone says.

I feel my throat tighten. I hope I'll like him.

The door opens and the smiling face that had been in the newspaper greets us, along with his blonde wife and little girl. I look him up and down and my eyes pop out. What is he wearing? I've never seen a man wear pants like that, lime green and yellow with pineapples on them.

I know they're moving here from Atlanta, but do other men there wear such pants? Maybe he plays golf or is wealthy. When I hear a few snickers beside me, I go underwater with my thoughts. I'm not ready to meet him and I don't think I can keep from staring at his bright-colored pants. I wish I could stay at the bottom of the pool until he and his family leave.

Some of my friends get out of the pool to meet them and ooh and aah over the daughter. I stay where I am. I'll skip the introductions, because I'm feeling like the little girl, who hides behind her mother's skirt. They don't visit long, so I don't think I'm being too rude.

The following Sunday is Dr. Curtis's first service. I sit in the back with my youth group friends. The pipe organ bellows out the hymn as we all stand to sing. I sneak a peek as our new priest walks by. He looks regal in his robes and his smile fills his face. The parishioners look at him, too, with smiles as wide as his. Maybe I will get through this transition too. I hate change, but my friends don't seem bothered.

I feel the power of his words during the sermon. Dr. Curtis is well educated and passionate. Maybe he isn't so bad. Maybe he's safe. If he's like he seems today, he may be great. Still, tears well up in me but don't fall.

"What do you think of him?" I whisper.

"I think he's cool."

The unshed tears lodge in my chest. I want to embrace change, but something holds me back every time. Fear? Of what? Being hurt? Not being safe? Whatever it is, I don't like it. I hate hearing the saying "Change is the only constant." I know it's true but change cripples me over and over. Perhaps it's because I have been bruised by it. Adults decide things for me, and I don't always like what they decide—like having one father leave me as an infant and another one when I was fifteen. I need things to stay the same, so I know what to expect.

# CHAPTER 33

One morning that summer, Ginger invites me to play backgammon with her and I promise to do so after softball practice. As I head to Barney and Brenda's for a visit, I crank up my car radio when Elton John's "Tiny Dancer" comes on. I'm excited Ginger asked me to play backgammon with her since these days I don't get much time alone with her. I know Moon will enjoy having her home tonight too.

I pull into Barney's driveway and am greeted by their dog, Sheba. Barney comes out when he hears her bark.

"I hope I'm not interrupting anything," I say.

"No," Barney replies. "We're just hanging out before practice."

"Ginger invited me to play backgammon with her when I get home. I'm surprised she and Mom aren't going out dancing."

"Where do they go?" Brenda asks.

"The Read House."

"Ah."

"Yeah, Mom and Ginger are sowing their oats. I think it's kind of funny, but they're happy."

"Well, Yog," Brenda says, "your mom has worked hard and hasn't had much of a chance to enjoy herself. The divorce has been hard on her."

"I know. I'm okay with it. It's just a little weird. She's acting years younger. The other night, my dad and his girlfriend showed up at the club. Mom told me that Ginger and their friend Ruth whistled at Mom while she and her partner showed off on the dance floor. It made Mom feel powerful."

Despite my words, I feel sadness. I wish it were my parents who were dancing together.

"Time to go, Yogi," Barney says, and stands up.

He and his daughter, Christe, head out in his truck, and I follow in my Datsun. On the field, the sun pelts us, making it feel like we're in a sauna. I'm glad I don't have to get behind the plate today. I convinced the coaches last summer to allow me to skip catching at practices. My sweat would cause the grainy dirt to stick to my skin and scalp. After practices, I want to hurry home and take a quick shower—not the kind that requires extra scrubbing.

Infield practice goes well. I hit a few deep balls during batting practice. Afterwards, Barney and C.E. lead us to a large oak tree. We sit under it in a semicircle.

"Girls, as you know, we have the state tournament coming up," C.E. says. "We have a good chance of taking it. If y'all play like you practiced today, there's nothing to worry about. You look solid."

Barney chimes in. "I've never coached a group of girls with this much talent. You gals know your stuff. You're hitting and fielding well. There's so much athleticism on this team."

I look around at my teammates—my friends. We do have a lot of talent. I have great pitchers who are throwing hard. I nod at Cathy, one of the pitchers, and she smiles back.

After the pep talk, I slide into my car, anxious to get home. I look at the clock and realize I'm running ten to fifteen minutes late. I hope Ginger, who doesn't like being by herself, waits for me. I'm reaching for my blinker to turn left into our subdivision when I pass Ginger. She has on her John Lennon sunglasses and a big grin. I wave at her, and she waves back. Her blonde hair whirls in the wind. Dammit. I'm too late. I feel my heart drop and I want to cry.

At home, I take a shower and let the warm water soothe me. I wish I hadn't been late. There's no telling where she's going. I bet some guy called her up and invited her over. Ginger would go at a moment's notice. I heat up two frozen meals and Moon and I eat in relative silence.

It's funny, I'm not sure where Mom is either. Maybe they're meeting each other, although Ginger didn't look dressed up. I hope she asks me to play backgammon again. Next time I won't be late. I climb in bed and fall fast asleep. The house is pitch black when I hear Mom hurrying down the hall. I sit up.

"Steph," she says as she opens my door and flips on the light.

I squeeze my eyes closed.

"Steph, listen. I have to go to the hospital. Ginger has had an accident."

"What? What type of accident?"

"I'm not sure. Erlanger Hospital called me to come right away."

I toss and turn the rest of the night. Brandon is at the fire hall. Moon has no idea something has happened to her mom. *Please God, don't let it be bad. Let her live.*

I fall asleep at some point. As soon as my eyes open, I creep down to Mom's room and ease her door open. Her sleeping face is frowning, and the room is messy, which isn't like her.

"Mom." I put my hand on her shoulder. "Mom."

She sits up looking startled.

"How's Ginger?" I ask.

Mom starts to cry and I feel my insides melt. My mouth goes dry. "What's wrong with her?"

"Shh," Mom whispers. "I don't want Moon to hear me. She broke her neck, Steph."

"How?"

"She dove into the shallow end of a hotel pool and snapped her neck."

I stand still. How could this happen? I feel like crying, but I can't. I need to be strong for Mom, for Ginger, for Moon.

"Steph, she's paralyzed from the neck down. She's in the ICU. She has screws in her head and a metal brace is keeping her neck in place."

I need to see her—put my hands on her. Comfort her somehow.

As if reading my thoughts, Mom says, "We can go see her at 11:00. That's the next visiting period."

Tears continue to slide down her face. "I dread telling Moon," she says. "Ginger wants me to tell her and then take her to her grandmother's place."

I feel like throwing up.

# CHAPTER 34

Colors fill our yard. May 2021 is putting on a show with her spring fling. Somehow the birth of life opens something inside of me as I sit in the backyard with the pups at my feet. The sun pushes back the darkness of the crazy Covid winter. Even though the pandemic is still front and center, new cases are beginning to slow down. I find my internal vulnerability beginning to shed its fears. I've made it this far without getting the virus. I'm facing my past head-on through writing and therapy. A sense of hope covers me as I hug my pups.

Writing below the surface forces me to reconnect with my true feelings. It's giving me a chance to hold up scenes from the past like a spinning globe. I can stop it wherever I want and look closely or from a distance. Feeling safe allows me to dig into the hard stuff and not crumble. I believe I'm going to get through Covid *and* through facing my past. I pick up the pups and go inside the house.

As our new home's construction moves forward, the need to empty out this one intensifies. I pull a stool to my dresser and continue the process of cleaning out unnecessary things. I don't want to take anything to our new house that we don't need or use. Reduce, reuse, recycle loops in my mind. Sometimes when I clean out something and Mike is unsure of letting it go, I say this mantra out loud.

I notice parallels to my life. I want to carve out the roots of my past so that I don't keep dragging them with me everywhere I go. I want to let go of the ball and chain that have bound me. I want to live in the present and wake up eager for what's next—not wake up afraid and feeling flawed. In the same way, I want to be intentional about how we use and fill our new home. I want to live in the beauty of the lake with an open heart and share the space with others.

The pups saunter in. Dusty yawns as I open another drawer. I find a sales ticket from a trip Mike and I made to Brazil a few years ago, which takes me back for a moment. I smile and put the ticket in the garbage sack beside me. Look, remember, let go. We're building a sustainable home, a home that works in harmony with the environment. I, too, want to live sustainably on the inside. Hope brings me closer to this dream. *Thank You, God, for the opportunity for new beginnings.*

Picking up a wedding picture of Mike and me, I rub the dust from the corners of the frame and put a hand on my heart. When I needed it the most, God gave me a gift I wasn't even looking for. What a story.

We were twenty-eight. He was a pediatric resident and I was a pediatric nurse at the children's hospital. We met in the newborn nursery. At the time, I was on the verge of traveling around the world.

"I need to get away," I told a friend. "I'm sick of the dating scene and of dysfunctional relationships."

"You have had a run of bad relationships," she agreed.

"Work is stressful, and I feel defeated. I don't even know what a lasting relationship will look like and what it will take for me to commit to a marriage. I think a new perspective on life is what I need."

One day I asked Cindy, another nurse, who Dr. Maley was. "Is he a man or a woman. Do you know?"

Cindy stepped around the corner from the nursery unit. I pointed to the resident's notes in a chart.

"I think Dr. Maley is a guy," she answered.

"Well, either way, he or she is going to be a good and thorough doctor. Have you read the notes?"

Cindy scanned the doctor's observations on baby Miller.

"Yeah, I see what you mean."

The next week, Cindy and I greeted the residents as they made their rounds to the newborn nursery. Their lab coats had their names sewn on. I knew most of these people from when I worked on the floor taking care of acutely ill patients. It was the new ones whose lab coats I searched. A young man with glasses, balding hair, and a beard and mustache walked in behind the group. *Dr. Maley*. Gotcha.

I hugged the residents I already knew and reached my hand out for his.

"Hey, Dr. Maley," I said. "I'm Stephanie Salmon. I'm one of the assistant head nurses."

He smiled. "Hi."

"I want you to know that you keep the best records of any resident I've ever seen. I think you're going to be a great doctor." I looked around at the others. "No offense, guys."

The residents laughed and began gowning and washing up before checking the newborns.

"Where are you from?" I asked Dr. Maley.

"Georgia."

My heart dropped a little. First, he's a doctor. Nope. Now he's from Georgia. Another no. I'm leaving the country soon anyway.

"I don't know many people from Georgia. I'm a Tennessee girl."

His hazel eye crinkled as he smiled.

Within a few weeks of working together, I could tell Dr. Maley was unique. He wasn't moody, no matter how tired he was. His kindness was genuine. One day he brought homemade chocolate chip cookies to the newborn nursery in a shoebox. "I can't thank you nurses enough for helping me collect stool specimens for my study."

We grabbed paper towels and devoured his treat. I'd never seen a resident take the time to bake cookies for nurses.

One day, I walked into the circumcision room to assist him. I strapped the baby's legs and arms down and held a pacifier in his mouth.

"You know," I said. "I'm going to be taking an eight-month leave of absence to travel. I'm looking to rent my house or sell it. I think you would like it."

"Tell me more about it."

When we finished the surgery, he tore off a paper towel and wrote down my phone number. I scooped up the dozing newborn and rocked him.

Dr. Maley smiled. "I'll call you and check it out on my next day off."

I smiled back and carried the newborn back to the nursery.

# CHAPTER 35

At the hospital with Ginger, I stand beside her bed but can't see her eyes. With clammy hands, I walk to the foot of her bed and do my best to smile.

"Hey, Ginger," I say. "Do you hurt?"

"Hey, Steph," her weak voice responds. "No, not too much. I can't feel anything from my chest down. This halo thing, though, gives me a headache."

Her blue eyes dart around the room like she's trying to find a way out. The confidence and whimsy are gone from her face. She looks frantic.

"Is there anything I can do for you?" I ask.

"Would you give me a sip of water?"

My heartbeat picks up as I look around for a cup of water, wondering how I'll manage it. I find a white Styrofoam cup with a straw in it. Her mouth tugs at it.

I can't believe I'm holding a cup of water for Ginger. How ridiculous is this? She's a grown woman. I'm just a teenager.

I stagger out of Ginger's ICU room. How could this awful thing have happened? This beautiful, athletic woman is now caged in a metal brace with screws in her head. She can't feel or move her legs, and she may never walk again. My heart hammers in my chest until my own head begins to hurt. She never would've left the house if I hadn't been late. It's my fault she had the accident. My stomach twists in knots.

I will do whatever I can for Ginger. I'll visit her every day and massage her limbs or do whatever she needs. I'll help take care of Moon. Maybe Ginger's feeling will come back. Maybe she'll be able to walk again.

I find a chair in the waiting room to wait for Mom, who is visiting with Ginger now. Nurses move in and out of the ICU rooms. A few doctors mingle around the desk area. I feel like an intruder. Even though I've been a hospital patient, I've never been in an ICU. I wonder how long they'll let Mom stay.

Life is so hard and unpredictable. How are we supposed to get through it? Who puts screws in a person's skull anyway? How is Moon going to take this news? I want to get out of here. *Come on, Mom.*

The familiar sterile smell penetrates my pores. I'm taken back to when I laid scared in a hospital bed. I shake off the thoughts and drop my head to my knees. I don't know how we're going to survive. *God, where are You? I can't feel You. I feel alone. I feel empty and sad. Ginger doesn't deserve this. Please help us. Please let Ginger walk again. Please help her. She isn't strong.*

A few minutes later, Mom, with tears in her eyes, joins me in the hall. She looks at me for answers, which makes me uncomfortable. I don't know what to do, so I pretend to be strong. I stand up and open my arms and let her cry. My stomach churns. *Keep it together, Steph. Be strong for your mom.*

"She looks awful," Mom whispers. "Doesn't she?"

"Yes," I answer. "The halo looks barbaric, but it's keeping her neck still."

Mom continues crying as we walk toward the elevators.

Maybe if we believe Ginger will be able to walk again it will come true. I cross my fingers behind me.

We are quiet while I drive us home. Mom will be talking with Moon before taking her to her grandmother's house. I'm thankful I don't have to do that.

As soon as we get home, I disappear into my bedroom, hoping to hide forever. I want Ginger's accident to go away. I feel so much pain and fear. If I had only been home on time. Can we fast-forward or go back in time?

Mom calls me to Moon's room. Mom is hugging Moon while she sits on the bed. The child, her head down, looks so small. I can see the glistening of tears on her cheeks. I don't know what to say. Finally, I tell her, "If you want to continue living here, I'll be happy to drive you when school starts."

"We'll see what her family wants for her," Mom says.

Both of us crowd around Moon as she packs. We can't do enough for her. I help carry her stuff to Mom's car and then I hold her close before she gets in. I have no soothing words to offer.

I close her car door and remain standing in the driveway long after they disappear.

# CHAPTER 36

The next day, I wake up and remember with sorrow Ginger's accident. She's not here. Moon is at her relative's house. The happiness in our home is gone. I shower and choke down Pop-Tarts and drive to volleyball practice. After practice, I head to the hospital—my eyes fixed on the road. I take a ticket in the garage and park my car. I step off the elevator, call the ICU ward, and wave at the nurses as I enter Ginger's room. One of them follows me to the side of her bed. She's the same one from yesterday.

"Since you want to help our patient here," she says, her eyes smiling at Ginger, "I'll show you some exercises you can do to help prevent foot drop."

I feel my heart rate increase. Maybe I *can* help Ginger get better. "I'm happy to do whatever you say."

"Thanks, Stephanie," Ginger says. Her voice sounds a little stronger.

The nurse shows me how to stretch Ginger's foot and I mimic her.

"It would really help," the nurse says, "if she had a pair of high-top sneakers to wear. The high-tops will help hold her foot in place in between therapy."

"I have a pair at home!" I squeal. "My basketball shoes."

"Stephanie, keep your basketball shoes," Gingers says. "I'll see if someone else can buy me a pair."

"No. I want you to have mine."

I feel happy when I leave the hospital. Not only can I do physical therapy on Ginger's feet, but I can give her my basketball shoes. *I just know she'll walk again and then move back in with us. Things will go back to the way they were.*

I return every day for the next week. I need Ginger to walk again. She won't be able to live with us if she's stuck in a wheelchair. Our carpeted floors and stairs will keep her out.

But by the next week, Ginger feels only the upper part of her chest and her arms. No changes since the accident. I'm working her feet when her doctor enters. As he asks her how she's feeling, I shrink back and decide I don't need to be in the room right now. Just as I make it to the door, Ginger calls out for me to stay. She says I'm family. I feel my face flush and return to her bed. I feel such a kinship with her too.

The doctor looks intently at Ginger. "I've spoken with some of my colleagues about your case. We don't think we can offer any more for you here. I've also been in touch with a neurosurgeon in Denver at the Craig Hospital. The hospital is renowned for working with quadriplegics like yourself. They teach people how to drive cars with their wrists as well as other life skills. Would you think about going there?"

This seems like great news to me! With these skills, she should be able to live with us. We can figure out the wheelchair issues later. Then I notice Ginger's frown.

"Why so far away?" she asks. "Isn't there a place closer?"

"I'm afraid not. Nothing in the area comes close to what they can do for you at Craig."

"Wouldn't that be cool if you could drive?" I say.

"Yeah. But it's far away. I don't know if my insurance will pay for that."

Not that I could help her out, but I don't care how much it costs if she can move back in with us. Maybe she'll learn how to cut hair with her wrists too. She's the best beautician I know.

"Just think about it for a day or so," says the doctor. "They have a bed waiting for you."

I notice Ginger isn't smiling. I wonder if she's getting depressed. After the doctor disappears from the room, I try to encourage her. "Just think, you could drive and come back to live with us."

She takes a deep breath and looks away. "Stephanie, I don't know what I'll be able to do. I don't know what to do."

*Please, Lord. Help Ginger make the right decision and go to Craig Hospital. Help her not be depressed. Thank You for the hope I feel.*

"Talk it over with Mom and your family. It sounds exciting. You'll know what to do."

I bend over and kiss her cheek. Her eyes don't meet mine. She seems in another world.

"I love you," I say. "I'll see you tomorrow."

"Bye, Stephanie."

I walk out feeling less hopeful. She must want this chance. *Please give her the desire to do whatever it takes to get better.* After getting my car, I drive straight to Barney and Brenda's. I need comfort because my heart feels heavy. I need Ginger to get better so she and Mom can have fun again. When Mom is having fun, I worry less.

Barney opens the front door and welcomes me. Brenda and Christe are in the den. We greet each other with hugs and Brenda turns the TV down.

"Ginger doesn't seem to want to try to get better," I tell them. "I keep believing she'll be able to walk again if she'd just stay focused. She needs to fight harder."

"She may be doing all she can," Brenda says. "You've said she isn't a strong person—at least not in an emotional sense."

"No, she isn't. But I need her back at home. We were having fun."

"I know, girl," Barney says. "But you might need to prepare yourself that she won't get better."

We talk some more about nothing, and then I decide I need to get home. My heart feels like it's cracking down the middle.

"I'll walk you out, Yog," Barney says.

The night is dark except for a lit lamppost beside my car. We stand at the back of it. When we hug goodbye, I don't want to let go. Instead, I try to kiss him, but he eases me away.

I'm mortified. I drive away, afraid I've messed up my relationship with Barney. What is wrong with me?

# CHAPTER 37

It's August 2021. My thirteen-year-old car rocks as I inch my way down our soon-to-be driveway. A deer stands in the dappled light in a small grove and we stare at each other as I pass. My heart skips a beat as our new house comes into view. The bold green paint and timber frame seem to look back at me and say welcome. *I don't deserve this place.* I shake away my thoughts as I get out of the car.

When Mike and I were checking the construction site together, we both hoped we would get to live here someday. I try to push my doubts away. *Will* we get to live here? Will we have enough money to pay for it? Or is there another shoe that will drop? I breathe in and remind myself of the thirty-one years I've had with Mike. My mind still tries to trick me into thinking I'm vulnerable to predators.

We've worked together to create this house, our final home. My breath catches every time I see it. *Thank You, God. Please help us use this gift to spread Your love to others.*

I walk inside to check out the newest changes and soak in the beauty. It's close to being done. The workers are putting in the trim in the great room while the painter is finishing in the basement. Everything looks amazing.

The sound of my steps echoes as I make my way upstairs to my future office. Windows fill three of the walls. As I watch from above, two wakeboard boats pass each other on the lake.

The deep sound of their engines becomes faint as I lose sight of them. I lean against a timber frame. The wood feels alive as I run my hand down the post. I can't wait to finish writing my memoir in this space.

This move, this change, feels like a beginning for me. Writing my way through my past is what I need to let go of its heavy burden. Change usually feels like the floor dropping out, but not this time. Curiosity is replacing fear. Change is losing its sting. I look around this beautiful room and take a deep breath. The past insecurity of questioning whether we will get to live here is fading.

This adventure began when I said *I do.*

I think about the night Mike came to my home in 1989. He was pretending to check out the house to see if he wanted to rent it while I traveled the world.

"Welcome, Dr. Maley," I greeted him. "Come meet my friends and join us for dinner."

"Please call me Mike."

He ate the meal I prepared and topped it off with dessert. *My kind of person.* The friends left shortly afterward.

"Do you want to see the rest of the house?" I asked.

"Not right now," he said. "Why don't we talk some more first?"

We talked and talked and talked. He listened too. At 1:00 a.m., we said goodnight. The next day, we sought each other out in the newborn nursery. My jaw had begun to hurt because of all the smiling I'd been doing.

"Hey, Steph," Mike said. "I have some tickets to J. Alexander's Restaurant. Do you want to come with me and check it out?"

Was he asking me out on a date?

"You want me to join you for dinner?"

"Yes."

"I'd love to."

He blushed and looked at his feet.

*Yes! He likes me too!*

I hated shopping but found myself buying a new outfit for our dinner date.

We met in front of the restaurant. His beard and mustache looked trimmed.

"Wow," he said. "I like your outfit."

"Thanks, it's new. Since I wear uniforms most of the time, I don't have a lot of other clothes. I'm glad you like it."

Our conversation flowed as we shared another meal together. I really liked him. *You're going around the world, Steph . . .*

I walk back downstairs and wish the men a good day. Before I drive away, I visualize all the fun we'll have with our family and friends. I look at the old barn left behind and wonder how we'll use it. My heart softens at the images. Happiness and refuge fill my vision. *May this space be a healing place for all who come.*

# CHAPTER 38

After a few weeks in the hospital that summer of 1979, Ginger leaves for Denver. She has agreed to give Craig Hospital a try. I stand by her bed and rub her arm as she cries.

"I'm scared, Stephanie," she says. "I don't want to be by myself."

"You will be surrounded by a lot of people who will help you get better," I answer. "Those strangers will become your friends. Don't you want to learn to drive again?"

"Yes, but I don't see how."

"Maybe not, but the doctors and nurses there will know how to help you."

"I guess so. I'm not looking forward to being so far from everyone I know."

"I'm going to pray for you and the staff every day. You can do this."

I wipe her tears with a tissue and squeeze her arm. I hate seeing her this way. I have to believe she'll get better. Other than my dad, no one dances as well as Ginger. She's like a queen on the floor. Her blue eyes smile at the audience as she dances with her strong legs and athletic body. I see her wearing the sequined white dress with a low-cut front—her face aglow. She's in charge, dazzling everyone. That memory makes my heart drop as I throw away the tissue.

I don't want her to feel my palms sweat, so I move to her feet. I wet a washrag and put soap on it and squeeze the water out over the sink. I replay our conversation. I want to smile at Ginger and convince her that everything will be all right. For a moment, I imagine myself floating near the ceiling. I look down on both of us in the room. My back is turned away from her. I look small. I see my teenage self—trying to be more than I am. Ginger looks tiny in the bed, but her halo looks huge. Her face is frowning and tearstained. *Help us, O Lord. Please.* I bring my attention back to the room and begin to wash her feet.

Ginger is airlifted on a Saturday morning. I said my good-byes the day before. Tonight, I feel lost, and find myself driving to Barney and Brenda's after dinner. Barney greets me when I knock on their front door. He has not treated me differently since I tried to kiss him. Softball practices erase my discomfort, and I know I can trust him and Brenda. *Thank You, Lord.*

"Hey, Yogi," he says. "How're you doing?"

I force a smile and say, "I'm fine."

My stomach is in knots. I feel lost because Mom is retreating again, and once again, our house is sad and quiet.

"You don't look fine. Come on in."

He and Brenda ask me questions about Ginger and my heart warms at their attention. I tell them as much as I know.

"I feel like I tricked Ginger," I say.

"How so, Yog?" Barney asks.

"I didn't tell her I heard her doctor talking to one of the nurses about Craig Hospital and how hard they'll work her. I encouraged her to go. I just want her to get better."

"Yogi, she's an adult and able to make up her own mind," Brenda admonishes.

"It's funny. Sometimes I don't feel like Ginger's an adult. She seems more like my age."

"Be that as it may, she's still an adult," Brenda says.

We watch a rerun of *The Andy Griffith Show* where Aunt Bee becomes a chef for a TV station. I love how simple life is in Mayberry.

I know I need to go home so I don't take up all their evening. I thank them for listening to me. Barney walks me to my car. The night air is warm and windy. Their streetlight is the only light on besides the glow of fireflies.

Sadness and neediness overwhelm me tonight, but I know I'm safe with Barney. I will not act on my emotions. Even if I did, he would not respond. I feel safe and happy knowing I can trust him. Tonight, I won't go home full of shame as I did last month.

My heart melts with gratitude that Barney has boundaries. I hope he and Brenda stay in my life. They feel like a safety net always ready to catch me when I fall. I don't know what I'd do if they weren't in my life.

# CHAPTER 39

It's August 1979. Don calls a few days after Ginger left for Denver.

"Hey, Steph. Do you want to come for a visit before school begins?"

"Sure," I reply. "But I need to see if it's okay to miss a few volleyball practices."

"Okay," Don says. "Call me back as soon as possible. Then I'll order your tickets."

"I will."

I hang up. A trip to Las Vegas may be fun. It'll help get my mind off Ginger. I keep thinking I need to head to the hospital and read to her. But she's gone. Our house is so quiet.

I call Mom at work to ask her about the trip. She agrees to it as long as Don is paying for the tickets.

I hang up and think about flying on a plane. I don't like takeoff or landing, but I guess I'll get through it by myself just as well as if I were sitting next to someone I know. This trip will also be the first time I visit my birth father without being forced. I guess I'm making progress.

Coach Williams teases me before giving me his blessing to travel. My senior year is coming up and I don't want to jeopardize my spot on the team.

Even though the flight to Las Vegas is smooth, I still grip the armrests as we take off and land. The passengers are loud and keep the flight attendants busy with drink orders. I'm more than ready to get off the plane when we get to the gate.

I call Don as he instructed me. He wants me to stand outside in front of the baggage claim area. A thermometer reads 115 degrees Fahrenheit, but it doesn't feel that hot. I guess it's the lack of humidity out here. I breathe in the air as I look for Don's convertible. Soon I see him coming my way. His long hair is windblown. His brown-rimmed sunglasses are large and look funny.

As he picks up my bags, he says, "I'm going to get us off the Strip. It'll take us twice as long to get home."

I'm a little disappointed but don't say anything. I tell him about Ginger as we drive to his and Joanna's home. I can't tell if he's listening or what he's thinking. I don't know him well enough to read him. The only comment he makes is to inquire about her paralysis. I guess that's the doctor side of him wanting to know the medical facts.

I settle into my bedroom across the hall from Michelle's room. A bass guitar remains in here, but most of the instruments are scattered around the house. Both Don and Joanna play.

I wouldn't have minded sleeping on their couch again—but for a week, I'm glad to have my own space. I sit on the full-size bed with the door closed. The long, shaggy carpet on the floor reminds me of the old carpet in my childhood bedroom.

My eyes scan the rest of the small room. Do I belong here? Don still feels like a stranger, but a familiar one. I like Michelle, but we are from different worlds. The South is nothing like her hometown of Sioux Falls, and Las Vegas isn't like any place I've ever been. I take a deep breath and decide to stop thinking.

Later that night, Michelle and I watch an episode of *The Untouchables* with Don and Joanna.

The next morning, I leave my room to find some breakfast. The smell of bacon fills the den. Don's cooking some and making eggs. I say yes when he asks if I want some.

As I sit at the bar stool, he asks a strange question. "Would you like to see jai alai this afternoon?"

"What's that?"

"It's a game played off three walls with a ball and basket throwers. The players are from the Basque Country in Spain. People bet on which team will win. I think you'd like it."

"Sounds like fun. I'd love to come."

"I have a few cases this morning and then I'll be free."

"Okay."

I guess he calls his patients *cases.* Or maybe that's what he calls surgery.

"One of these mornings, if you'd like, you can come with me to surgery."

Can he read my mind? "Really? That'd be cool."

Don returns after lunch, and we drive to the MGM Casino. As we step inside, muted noise wraps around us. People sit at slot machines while others sit around tables where dealers spin wheels. I follow Don to the back part of the casino to the jai alai court.

Four players are on the court warming up. A huge net acts as a wall. My eyes try to keep up with the speed of the ball.

"Sit wherever you want," Don says. "I'm going to get a drink and place my bets. Do you want anything?"

"Sure. I'll take a Coke."

I watch the players. I've never seen anything like this game. I'm mesmerized when Don returns with my Coke and his drink.

"Cheer for the blue team," he says. "I put my money on them."

I guess gambling knows no ends here. It seems like everything is up for betting on.

Between each set, Don explains the game to me. He also buys an alcoholic drink between each game.

I ask him about it when he returns for the fifth time. "Are you an alcoholic?"

He laughs. "No. These drinks are watered down so that there's hardly any alcohol in them."

I don't trust his response but don't say anything further. We have fun the rest of the day. Then he invites me to go gambling with him and I agree.

That night, we return home after Don plays blackjack for several hours. He drinks throughout the evening. It's midnight when he picks up a guitar. "You are my sunshine, my only sunshine," Don sings to me.

I've never had anyone sing to me. I feel his love for me in his music and the time he's spending with me. Maybe he's not so bad.

The next morning, I knock on Michelle's door and ask her if she wants to go out on the town that night.

Her eyes look down. "I'm not sure what you mean."

"What if we tried to get into a bar? We could dress up to look older than we are."

"Oh, I don't know. You have to be twenty-one."

"Oh, in Tennessee, eighteen is considered the legal age." I shrug. "Let's go have some fun anyway."

I hound Michelle all day until she gives in. When we make it home later that night, I stare at the ceiling with the lights off, incredibly embarrassed. I managed to get us kicked out of Circus Circus, be turned away from three bars, and then not be able to pay our bill at the bar we *were* able to get into. Michelle will never trust me again. Don will be furious.

"Dad is going to be angry," Michelle told me when we pulled into the driveway. "He's not a good angry."

In the dark room now, I pull the covers over my eyes and try to sleep, but the questions keep coming. Why are you here? Do you belong? Why does Don matter to you now? Why did you force Michelle to go along? I shouldn't have lied to the security guard at Circus Circus and pretended to be twenty-one. I'm only seventeen and I'm sure I look it. But her threat to me to either see the manager or leave challenged me.

After the guard refused to let us in, I turned to Michelle. "Why don't we check out upstairs?"

"We have to leave, Stephanie," Michelle pleaded. "Didn't you hear her? We have to leave."

She looked so scared as I started to walk upstairs, but I was angry. I wanted to be in control. But the noise in the children's area was even louder, so we left and tried one more bar. When we were welcomed inside, I ordered us mai tais. When the bill came, we were three dollars short. I would've had the money if I hadn't spent it on the slot machines at Circus Circus—where I got caught.

I fall asleep with a pit in my stomach.

# CHAPTER 40

It's September 2021. With fresh eyes, I walk through our twenty-one-year-old home in Toccoa. Sold. I still can't believe it. Our dream of moving into the new lake house is becoming a reality.

I can still hear our young boys running through this house with their friends. Their laughter was like a balm. I smile as I grab a box, return to my bedroom, and open a drawer.

We built this house so we could raise our growing sons in a neighborhood. But I have pined for the lake ever since we sold our nine-hundred-square-foot home on the water. It was Mike's and my first house when we moved here. I wonder if we'd be moving back to the lake if we could have kept that small house—the one we had to sell to help pay for this house. Who knows?

Quiet snores from the pups make me think of them when they were young. Thirteen years ago, they were tiny and full of energy. My heart softens at the memories. Such life lived here. I think of all the people who have passed through our home. *Thank You, Lord. Thank You for Your love. Thank You for the gift of memories. I love You.*

I stand up to stretch and run through all the things I need to do today: buy more wrapping tape, get more boxes, pay bills, and keep emptying the house for the upcoming move. We must be out by September 18—only two more weeks. The pups stir, I lift them from the bed, and they follow me to the kitchen. I grab their leashes from the hook in the laundry room and guide Dusty off the kitchen steps as we head outside. The sun feels like a comforting blanket.

I'm so lucky. All these years of battling the past and now I'm finding relief. Even with the new house and the move, I don't feel as frenetic as I once did. I don't wake up with dread every day. When I do, I shake off the feeling right away. I hug myself, enjoying the quiet around me.

Covid-19 is a shield that allows me permission to step out of my hurried life. A shield I hope to hold onto when the virus passes. As the dogs and I walk, the slight breeze cools my skin. I tilt my head back and close my eyes. Dusty and Rascal pull on the leash. Annie, our outdoor dog, is ready to get in the creek.

When we return home, the pups drip with water. Annie shakes her coat, leaving small pinprick patterns on the asphalt. I feel like I've been shaking off my past ever since I married Mike. He is the most loving person I know. His support is like one big deep breath. I'm the luckiest person in the world to be married to him.

My drinking days ended sometime between Mike's visit to my house and our wedding day. I had so much respect for him, I didn't want him to see me drunk. It's not one of my better sides. Communication replaced the attempts to dull my pain with alcohol. *Thank You, God.*

When I met Mike, I kept triple sec, vodka, rum, gin, tequila, sweet and sour mix, and cola on a bottom shelf in my small, wood-paneled kitchen. My drink of choice was a Long Island Iced Tea, introduced to me when I was eighteen and living in Las Vegas. A group of Scottish people had come to visit a friend of my dad's, and they took me to lunch.

The restaurant was low lit. I sat on a curved couch with five adults, tracking their conversation with ease. I had just spent two weeks giving the two women a trip around Southern California. I think I will forever be able to identify a Glaswegian accent.

"What will you have to drink?" a waitress asked.

As they placed their orders, I could tell that they were up to something.

Iain pointed to me and said, "She'll have a Long Island Iced Tea."

The waitress didn't pause or question my age. The others were all in their twenties or older.

I ate my club sandwich and lapped up every drop of the tea. My new friends laughed when I tried to stand up. They helped me outside into the bright sun and hot temperatures. That drink stayed with me for the next ten years—along with vodka tonic.

Those days are over.

I unleash the dogs and put them on the couch. Brooke will be calling me soon. Teletherapy has worked out so well.

On the call, I tell Brooke how reflecting on my life while I pack up the house has been cathartic.

"How so?"

"I just wrote about Ginger and her accident. Do you remember that story?"

"Yes. What happened to her?"

"She didn't get any better at the rehabilitation hospital in Denver, and her care suffered when she returned to Chattanooga. Her medicines caused her to have such severe spasms, she would end up on the floor. I'd visit her at this small, non-handicapped apartment and feel frustrated and overwhelmed. It was depressing. It was like she was dumped off and left alone."

"What are you feeling right now?"

"Sadness. Somehow I felt responsible for her care. I guess it was the enabling part of me. Home health nurses came to see her but didn't stay with her. She couldn't do much of anything for herself, and Ginger's family didn't have a lot of money.

"And why did you think Ginger was your responsibility?"

"Back then, a little old lady could be walking across the street and trip and somehow I thought it was my fault. Focusing on someone else's problems meant I wouldn't have time to look at my own. Of course, I didn't understand any of that at the time and wasn't conscious of my warped thought process. The pain from visiting with Ginger became so intense I stopped going. I hid behind the fact I was in nursing school, working multiple low-paying jobs, and so on. It's like I rode off into the sunset. But there was a time when Ginger was getting better care. When that happened, I would arrange to have a wheelchair at church and take her there. I don't remember how long that lasted."

"Do you see how her care was not your responsibility? And you were, what, eighteen, nineteen?"

"Yes, but I didn't see it at the time. I felt a lot of guilt and paralyzing frustration."

I pause for a moment. After a deep breath, I tell Brooke more about Ginger.

"She lived another thirteen years or so after her accident. Back then, I wanted to fix her so she could continue to live with us. Mom and Ginger were so happy before the accident."

We look at each other and sit in silence. I appreciate these moments. There's no glossing over the pain.

Finally, Brooke says, "You took a lot on in your teenage years after your parents' divorce."

"Yeah. I see that now. I wanted Mom to be happy. Of course, I now know that was not for me to do—not that I could anyway."

After teletherapy, I return to packing. With another box in hand, I head to my room. *You are with me always, Lord. I feel Your presence and strength.*

# CHAPTER 41

Las Vegas, 1979. As soon as I wake up and open my eyes, I remember last night's events. It wasn't a bad dream. I roll over and stare at the wall. I wonder how mad Don will be when he finds out I couldn't pay the bar bill. Michelle warned me he can get super mad. I feel my muscles tense just thinking about his reaction. I wonder if he will still like me after I tell him. Just as I rinse out my cereal bowl, I hear the garage door open. Don's home. I feel the pit in my stomach drop lower. The kitchen door opens and Don greets me as he walks in.

While he makes his breakfast, I sit on a stool and watch him cook. I need to get last night off my chest. He's in a good mood. Maybe he won't be too mad.

"Um, Don," I start. "I got Michelle and me into a bar last night and when the bill came, I was three dollars short."

His shoulders pull up. He turns around to face me. "Stephanie, you're not in Chattanooga." His voice drops in tone and his frown stops me cold. "I can't believe they let you leave."

"The waitress was real nice," I say. "I told her I'd pay her back."

"I don't care what she said! This is Las Vegas, where the mafiosa still live and reign. There are bodies buried in the desert and in Lake Mead that will never be found. You can't mess around here. Don't. Ever. Do. That. Again."

"Yes, sir." I feel horrible.

He moves the pan to the side, grabs his keys, and tells me to hurry up. "We're heading over there right now so you can pay her back. You were very lucky."

I look at the clock and worry the waitress won't be there. Are bars open in the morning?

I remain quiet as I slide in next to Don. He punches the remote for the garage door and whips the car in reverse.

I guess he doesn't like me anymore. I blew it. All these years out of my life and now I've disappointed him.

When we get to the bar, he hands me a twenty-dollar bill.

"It was only three dollars," I remind him.

"She deserves a tip for being nice to you and Shelley and for trusting you'd be back."

Twenty dollars? That's a lot more than three. *Please be open. I don't want to go through this humiliation again.* I get out and walk toward the small building. It looks so different in the daytime.

The door is unlocked. I see a man with a mop.

"Excuse me," I mumble. "Is the waitress who worked last night here?"

"Do you mean Carla? Brown-headed?"

"Yes, sir."

"No, but she's a good friend of mine. What do you need?"

"I just want to give her this money. I wasn't able to pay for all of my drinks last night."

He smiles and takes the twenty. "I'll make sure she gets it."

"Thank you so much."

I feel like running. My heart is beating a mile a minute. I climb back into Don's car. "She wasn't there, but a friend of hers was and said he'll give her the money. I believe him."

"You can't trust everyone," Don says. "You are not in the South anymore. Things are different here."

"Yes, sir."

"And I'm tired of you calling me Don. Will you call me Dad instead?"

At this moment, I'll agree to anything to avoid seeing his angry eyes.

"Sure, Dad."

His features soften. "Thank you."

"Thank you for the money. I'm sorry I wasn't able to pay her."

"We'll forget about it this time. Just don't do it again."

"I won't."

"How about I teach you how to play squash? I think you'll do well with it."

"Squash? I've never heard of it. What is it?"

"You play with a racquet and a small ball in a small room. It's similar to racquetball but harder and faster."

"Sure. I'd love to give it a try."

I feel like I'm walking on eggshells with the need to please Don and make him happy. Something has shifted in our relationship. I want him to be proud of me as his daughter. Just a year ago I didn't want to come out here and see him. Now, he matters to me. I feel like a fish on two lines, a daughter with two dads. Part of me wants to unhook myself from Don's line and go back to having only one father.

# CHAPTER 42

It's September 1979. With my school schedule in hand, I trot up the stairs to begin my senior year. I can't wait to see Coach Finnegan and my friends. When I see him at the top of the stairs, my palms begin to sweat.

"Hey, Yogi," he says, smiling.

"Hey, Coach Finnegan." All of a sudden, my mouth feels stuffed with cotton.

"How was your summer?" he asks.

"Great. How 'bout yours?"

"It was good. I've been looking forward to coming back."

"Me too."

"I'm teaching some senior electives this year. Check them out."

"I will." I hope he can't hear my heart beating. I need a drink of water and fast.

The bell rings.

"I'll see you around, Steph."

"You too."

I run down the hall to my first class, grabbing a sip of water as I pass the water fountain. I smile all the way to my seat. I'm so happy I ran into Coach Finnegan. I will make sure I take any class he offers.

After school, Coach Williams passes out our volleyball schedule. St. Andrews?!

"Coach," I say, "we get to play in Sewanee?"

"Fish, it says so on the schedule. I guess we will."

"Cool. We need to stop at a restaurant while we're there. It's called Shenanigans."

"We'll talk about that when we get closer to playing there."

This year's going to be great. I can't wait to show Sewanee to my friends.

A month later, we climb into the school's green van and begin the hour-long trip to St. Andrews, followed by some of our parents. I haven't been up to Sewanee since Andy's graduation.

He called the other day to check on me. Near the end of the conversation, he said that *we* have a song that describes our relationship.

"Do you know the song 'Can We Still Be Friends' by Todd Rundgren?" he asked.

"Maybe."

"Well, pay attention to the lyrics the next time you hear it."

"Okay."

Remembering the call, my stomach feels rocky. I move up to the front of the van where Coach Williams is. I talk about the Episcopal college and the mountain. *We're going to my territory.* My Catholic friends listen to me as I describe how beautiful it is where we're going.

"And Shenanigans is the coolest place," I say. "There's writing on the walls, and the floor is old and uneven. They have a sandwich called the Shenaniwich that's piled high with meats and alfalfa sprouts."

"Alfalfa sprouts," says one of my teammates. "Yuck."

I laugh. By the time we arrive at St. Andrews, I'm talked out.

"Fish," Coach says. "Can we focus on volleyball now?"

"Yes, sir," I answer with a smile.

We win our games and pile back into the van with high spirits.

"Coach," I say. "Can we please eat dinner at Shenanigans?"

"Yes, Fish, we're going. The parents are coming too."

I feel like a proud parent as I push away the memories of coming here with Andy and usher everyone into my favorite restaurant. I want new memories. As I show Mom around, I can tell she is less enthused by the restaurant.

"Stephie, what kind of place is this?" she says.

"Mom, the food is great. It's a cool place. They don't even use ice in their drinks."

"I've never heard of a place not serving ice."

"I promise. You'll like it."

I walk to my friends and watch them take in the menu that is handwritten behind the counter.

After we pick up our orders and sit down at well-used tables, Coach Williams finds me.

"Fish, I'm drinking out of a jar with no ice."

I smile and know he's teasing me.

I'm almost too excited to eat my food. To share this place with my friends is so cool. Even though it is only an hour away from home, it is still out of town. What a gift. I look across the street at the hardware store where Andy worked part-time. The stories I could tell but won't.

I return my focus to my friends. I feel safe being here with all of them. We laugh and talk about our wins. Our team is better this year. We Lady Knights may make a name for ourselves.

After we finish eating, we load up into the van again. "Fish," says Coach Williams. "I enjoyed my meal. Everything was good except for the lack of ice."

Giggles fill the van as we head home. I look out the window and think about how Coach Finnegan graduated from the University of the South. Another happy thought about Sewanee. I feel attracted to this beautiful place on the one hand while feeling shame on the other. I smile at my friends and tuck away thoughts of Andy. I want to hold onto this special day.

Later, I hear Todd Rundgren's "Can We Still Be Friends" on the radio:

> We had something to learn, now it's time for the wheel
> to turn.
> Things are said one by one, before you know it's all
> gone.
> Let's admit we made a mistake, but can we still be
> friends?
> Heartbreak's never easy to take, but can we still be
> friends?

No, and you're the one who made the mistake.

# CHAPTER 43

September 2021. Tomorrow is moving day. Packing, throwing, and giving away, our home consists of boxes and space. The hardwood floors show scratches and stains from our time here. Memories are locked away in our minds.

I scan my room for some hidden tidbit from the past. Does it stay or go away? I match this cleansing in my mind. What do I keep and what do I leave behind? Am I ready to let go of the past?

As I walk through the house, my steps are pronounced as I move upstairs. I go through the boys' rooms. *I'm so thankful we weren't raising them during these Covid times. They would have been home anyway but kept from playing with their friends.*

How strange to stare into their empty closets that once held hundreds of Legos and other toys. *Life is fast. Hold on to what you have.* Or is it more about enjoying the life in front of you while taking what you like and leaving the rest?

I love the life we lived here. This history is what I want to hold onto and remember. I look down at the backyard where our children spent hours jumping on their trampoline and playing with their friends. These are the images I want to relive.

When I hear the dogs stirring downstairs, I return to the main floor. Rascal comes to me with a wagging tail. I sit on the floor beside him and Dusty and rub their coats. We held a wedding in this room years ago. Oh, and a New Orleans–themed party—complete with crawdads. I smile and drop my shoulders. I know Mike and I will create new memories at our new home, so I suspect I won't miss this place too much. Living here is what we needed to do for our children. The neighborhood was a safe place to raise them.

All this change and still my mind and body act like it's as easy as taking my next breath. I know having both doses of the Moderna vaccine is giving me peace of mind too. Mike and I are vaccinated and will get a booster when it's time. Perhaps moving to the lake, the place I've longed to be, erases all of my usual fears. The move is more important than the unknown—and Mike and I created this future space together. Maybe that's enough.

I take a deep breath and feel grateful to be moving in with a friend of ours, Lisa, until our place is ready. I know Mike and I will have fun during this transition. I love Lisa. She and I say what we mean and mean what we say and aren't mean when we say it. I value this trait. Secrets and holding back the truth don't serve me anymore. Being a scribe to my past secrets diminishes their sting.

Lisa has stayed hunkered down at home like me. I think the biggest adjustment will be just being around someone all day.

Annie, our outdoor dog, barks. I look out the window and see Mike's car pull in.

When he comes into the house, we hug and kiss. Annie wags her tail on my leg.

We step in the kitchen, where we're greeted by the smell of pesto. This room is the last one we need to pack up.

"Hungry?" I ask.

"Yes. I'll get the plates."

I smile and feel grateful to have him by my side. I'm so thankful I said yes.

# CHAPTER 44

1979, senior year. I love being at school. The bell calls us to class. Lockers slam as we hurry to our next room. I breathe in the smell of the hallways as I head to Coach Finnegan's classroom. I managed to squeeze in his elective course. My heart hammers in my chest as I slide into my desk.

He smiles at me and addresses the class. "Has anyone ever read or heard of the book *Anna Karenina*?"

Heads turn as we look for someone who read this book. I've never heard of it. No hand raises.

"That's all the better," he says. "The Russian author, Leo Tolstoy, wrote this novel in 1878. It's considered one of the greatest pieces of literature. Reading the book and analyzing it will take up most of the semester. It's over eight hundred pages long."

I don't think I've ever read anything that long. I don't care. If he likes this book, then I'll like it too.

Coach Finnegan passes each of us a copy. Wow. The paperback is quite thick. I smell the fresh pages. I look over the cover with its bright colors of pink and red with a woman and a man standing next to each other looking away. I'm impressed that Coach is going to teach us about this story; it looks more like a college-level book. I see some of my classmates making faces at their copies. I think they regret taking the class. If I didn't have such a crush on Coach, I'd probably join them.

I'm so happy to be a senior, but I realize it means I won't be here with my friends next year. We'll go our separate ways. When I think about graduating, my stomach knots up. I love my friends and playing sports. I need to focus on the present and enjoy every minute, but I wish the year could go on forever.

As I walk down the hall to my next class, I begin to look hard at the walls and windows and lockers. I don't want to forget one thing about this place. Next summer could also be my last season of fast-pitch. I won't get to play softball anymore unless I try to get into the professional women's league.

I go into my class with a head full of present and past worries. I do my best to listen to Miss Bevins, my Math IV teacher. I squeeze my pencil between my thumb and two fingers, take a deep breath, and do my best to take in a new formula. Shoot. I'll even miss Miss Bevins.

At the end of the day, I race to the locker room to change for volleyball practice. Coach Williams expects us to be on the court within five minutes. He acts tough but he's a softy.

I pull up my knee pads and once again curse change. Just when life seems to be going well, it changes. Why can't the good parts last longer than the bad ones?

My tennis shoes skid on the floor as I push through the door and trot down the stairs to the basketball court. The net is already set up. I realize that this Halloween will be our last time to roll Coach Williams's yard. Man. I'm making myself sad. I shake my head to try and empty my thoughts.

"Fish," Coach yells. "Look out, here comes the ball. You need to get your head out of the clouds."

The ball doesn't make proper contact on my wrists and goes sailing off. After that mistake, I think only about practice. *Thank You, Lord, for sports.* Competition feeds my soul. I love the comradery with my teammates. When I'm focused on sports, nothing else gets in. I'm not hustling for love or dwelling on past betrayals. I'm my truest self. I don't feel hungry for love or much of anything else.

# CHAPTER 45

Halloween night. Four of us brave the cold night in Debbie's Jeep as we head to Coach Williams's house. The Jeep's heater is no match for the frigid air.

"Coach says he's ready for us this year," I yell over the noise. "Makes me a little nervous about tonight."

"He's bluffing," Debbie shouts.

"We'll know soon enough," Mary replies. "We're almost there."

Debbie slows down as we turn on his street. She cuts the lights and pulls into his driveway. We drop out of the Jeep. Nervous giggles escape my throat. As I open the gate to his backyard, I hear a noise. A puffball comes running towards me. Oh my gosh, he has a dog.

"Guys, look," I whisper. "Coach Williams has a puppy."

Debbie, Angie, and Mary stop what they're doing and come pet the pup. The little guy grabs my toilet paper and takes off running. The dewy ground pulls shards of paper from his mouth. I cover my mouth as the puppy drags the toilet paper through the backyard as Mary locks the gate. We fly around like happy witches on brooms.

We return to the front and begin soaping the windows of Coach's car. All of a sudden, the front door opens and Coach comes crashing down the steps. He reaches to his right and snatches a hose off the ground. We scream and dive toward

Debbie's Jeep with water spraying everywhere. I see him run to Debbie's side and point the hose inside the Jeep. I hate cold water, so I take off across the street. I hear Debbie, Angie, and Mary shrieking while Debbie puts the Jeep in gear.

I look back and see the white T-shirt of Coach Williams running in my direction. I laugh and shake at the same time as I try to find a place to hide. The streets run parallel with the small homes nestled close to each other. I cut across another street and turn one more time. I stop to gulp for air, but *he's still chasing me!*

I can't believe Coach hasn't given up on finding me. Is he upset with us? I'm not sure this night is fun anymore, but he's not going to catch me. I slip into someone's garage. Light spills from their kitchen, where I hear voices talking. *Oh my gosh.* What if someone opens the door and finds me in here? Am I breaking the law?

It's darker in here than outside, so I sneak a peek around the wheel of a car. I see Coach walking by with his white shirt as bright as a lantern. I pull back and hold my breath and wait for what seems like forever. Then I slip outside and make my way back towards his house, hiding behind bushes. Did Debbie and the others stay around and wait for me somewhere? I hope they aren't too mad at me.

As I slink across another yard, I see Debbie's Jeep sitting at the end of the road. I take a deep breath and run. When I get into the car, I realize that I'm not the only one shaking. The heater is turned up full blast and I see droplets of water on the floorboard.

"Thanks for not leaving me," I say as I close the door.

"Well, I thought about it," Debbie huffs. "You ran off and didn't get wet at all."

"I know. I'm sorry."

"Boy, Coach Williams was dead set on catching us this time," Mary says.

"He chased me two streets over," I tell them. "I was terrified. I thought he'd quit after a little while, but he didn't." I pause for a moment. "He seems mad this year. When I was hiding, I kept thinking, *what's he going to do to me if he catches me?*"

We ride back to Debbie's home in silence. I keep replaying seeing Coach Williams walking by the garage in his white T-shirt. My heart begins to pound again because that's the first time I felt afraid of him. If he had caught me, would I have yelled and alerted the family that I was in their garage? I hope I would have used my voice.

I know Coach isn't like Andy, but maybe he has an angry side. At school, he's a cutup, so I bet he's just in a bad mood. That's all.

# CHAPTER 46

It's almost October 2021 and time for our family Zoom call. Mike and I sit on Lisa's couch with the pups between us. We are so lucky she opened her home to us. Faces begin to appear one by one. On the screen, Michael's Hawaiian background is full of sunshine and surfboards, while Matthew sips his wine in Atlanta as he stretches out on his bed.

Mom speaks first. "I can't help but think of Lisa and how it must be for her to have you live there. Two adults and three dogs added to her home. Poor thing."

"Mom," I reassure her, "we're enjoying our time together. I promise."

"Pat," Mike says, "Lisa and Steph spend most of their time laughing. We're getting along well."

Lisa comes in from the other room and squeezes in beside us. She leans in front of Mike's iPad.

"Hey, Pat," Lisa says. "They're telling the truth. I love having them here. It's fun. Plus, they take out the trash and empty the dishwasher before I can turn around. Don't worry about me. All is good."

"Well," Mom replies, "I just know this situation has to be hard on you."

Everyone laughs at Mom's determination to deem our time together as nothing but torture for Lisa. We shake our heads and move the conversation to Covid. The numbers are decreasing in our area and in Hawaii.

"We can't wait to see you in October, Michael," I say. "By the way, what is today?"

"It's September thirtieth," Matthew answers.

"We've been at Lisa's for two weeks? Time flies. And we leave for Hawaii on October seventeenth. That's only three weeks away. I sure hope our home isn't ready until we get back."

"I doubt it will be," says Mike.

I take a deep breath and lean into him. I'm not fearing the upcoming move or even taking a trip during this transition. I miss Michael and need to put my hands on him. I don't know if it's all the writing I'm doing or what, but I feel like I'm sitting in God's palm. A sense of peace enfolds me inside and out.

The sound of everyone's voices brings me back to the moment. I look at their beautiful and handsome faces. I want to memorize them. They are my world. I wish Mom lived closer but feel grateful for Zoom. Even though we live apart, being able to see each other in real time is priceless.

I'm happy the others agreed to try Zoom. I want our family to be close. With Michael living in Hawaii, I thought these video calls would be a good way for all of us to stay connected. In a way, Zoom is giving us a glimpse into each other's lives. Michael took us on a walk to the beach when he first moved to Oahu and I felt that I was walking right beside him. I imagined the smell of the ocean and the feel of the breeze. Matthew and his roommate's cats also entertain us on calls.

After Michael heads off to the beach before going to work and Mom signs off to rest for a while, Mike and I spend some more time with Matthew before we get off the call. My heart feels warm. As Mike and I hold hands, with the dogs asleep beside us, I am grateful for our family and God's love. *Thank You!*

Mike, Lisa, and I retreat to the TV room and settle on the couch and love seat. Lisa turns on the TV to *Ted Lasso.*

For a moment I think about our conversation with Mom and our sons. I need to let go of trying to get Mom to understand. If she wants to worry about Lisa, my choice has to be to let her. I know Mom has close friends, but I wonder if they feel free to say whatever is on their minds.

I tune into the show and lean against Mike.

# CHAPTER 47

It's midwinter of my senior year of high school; I unfold the mail and read my SAT scores. Terrible. *I'll never make it into the University of the South with these scores.* I hate standardized tests since I've never done well on them.

I plop down on my bed and feel a knot grow in my stomach. I dread telling our new priest, Dr. Curtis, who is so supportive and has been helping me pursue college. I've known I would go, but he's pushing me to reach higher. I want to attend Sewanee as a pre-med student, but *not with these scores . . .*

On Sunday, I find Dr. Curtis at church and join him for breakfast. I hope all the background noise in our parish hall will drown out my words.

"Well, I got my SAT scores this week."

"How did you do, Stephanie?"

"Not very well. I think my dog could have done better."

"I doubt that. What was your total score?"

I tell him and his eyes widen.

"That's terrible."

One of the things I love about him is his honesty, which today is painful.

Ashamed, I add, "I don't do well on standardized tests."

"You aren't alone, though I'd hoped you would do better than that. Sewanee is tough to get into."

"I know. I guess I need to look elsewhere."

I stare at my plate of doughnuts and bacon, but I'm no longer hungry.

"Stephanie, you have so much to offer. They will be lucky to have you. The admissions board just needs to be shown that." He smiles at me. "You have so many extracurricular activities at school and at church. Your grades are good. These things will be in your favor."

"I hope so. I wish everything didn't depend so much on SAT scores."

"I'll write a letter to Sewanee about you and will ask Buckley and Jimmy to do the same. Or you can ask them."

Since the University of the South is an Episcopal college, maybe letters from several of my priests will make the difference. "Thank you, Dr. Curtis."

"We'll do our best for you. You're a gem. They need to know that."

At school the next day, everyone who took the SAT is going around comparing scores. I keep mine to myself. I'm too embarrassed.

The school year is going by so fast. Basketball season is about to start and I'm running out of time with Coach Finnegan. My crush on him grows stronger each day. What will I do when school is over? I can't bear to think I won't see him anymore.

The bell rings and I hustle to my elective class on death and dying. Reading Dr. Kübler-Ross's book has been eye-opening. Miss Tingle, our teacher, questions us about our latest chapter.

At one point, a classmate raises her hand. "Do you think people who are unconscious can really hear people talking to them?" she asks.

"Well, Dr. Kübler-Ross has found that to be the case."

I think about the stages of grief—denial, anger, bargaining, depression, and acceptance. I know I have experienced these emotions. I imagine Dr. Kübler-Ross knew that unconscious people could hear others talking to them. It makes total sense even though we don't know how the spirit moves. God does, and I think He would open the ears of someone dying to hear their loved ones saying goodbye.

After class I run into Mary and we whine together about the year ending. We are not ready to move on.

Of course, Mary doesn't know I may not get into the one college I want to go to or how I feel about Coach Finnegan. She probably wouldn't like it that I have such strong feelings for a teacher. I wish I felt I could trust her with this emotion, but trust doesn't come easy for me and I don't want to risk losing my friendship with her.

Our new head basketball coach, a woman, learned I have asthma. During our game that night, as I dribble past her, she yells, "Fish, do you need to come out?"

My face feels hot and my lungs feel like they are going to burst, but I shake my head at her. The next thing I know, I am being taken out of the game.

I hate asthma and looking weak. I think of the stages of grief and know that the effects of asthma cause me grief. I'm stuck in anger. I want my body to perform no matter what I put it through. Running full court challenges me every time. If we still played half court, if I didn't have asthma, I know I would be a top scorer, as I was in elementary school. At least softball doesn't require me to run at full throttle. I wonder if that is another reason it's my favorite sport.

I glare at the back of my coach's head, but I know she did me a favor. I was out of gas. On the bench, I gulp air and hope she'll put me in again. Crashing my SAT scores left me feeling dumb, so I don't like feeling weak at basketball too.

# CHAPTER 48

Andy calls to chat for a minute. I clench my jaw.

"How are you doing?" he asks.

"Good. I love school, my friends, and playing sports. We're about to finish basketball season."

"I'm glad school is going well for you. You need that."

*What do you know?*

He prattles on. "I watched a movie the other day called *The Goodbye Girl.* It has Richard Dreyfuss in it. He was in *Jaws.* Remember?"

"Yeah."

"There's a part in the movie where he pulls panties off a shower rod and gives the other character an earful. It made me think of us. It was funny."

I turn as if to keep from hearing this information. I will never watch this movie. Yuck.

He continues trying to get me to talk. Instead of listening, I go back to my last time with him in Mississippi. I'm so glad he didn't touch me. Maybe those days are over. I wish I could tell Mom about him, but where would I even begin? I can't and won't—she would crumble. I won't be responsible for adding any more stress to her life.

# CHAPTER 49

It's October 2021. The sun warms my face as Mike and I walk to church from Lisa's; she lives just a few blocks away. His hand caresses the back of mine as the voices of the choir drift toward us. Our church built an outdoor pavilion during the pandemic so we can meet in person. How good it is to be able to hear our service from down the road. When we arrive, I remain cautious and sit an extra six feet away from everyone.

It's still warm enough for me to slip off my shoes. I close my eyes and listen to the words of the liturgy. Mockingbirds call to each other across the pavilion. Several heads turn to see who's making the ruckus. A breeze eases the warmth. It's fall but still feels like summer. After the Old Testament reading, we sing a camp song. I hear an airplane take off from our small airport a few miles away and twist my neck to follow its ascent.

Mike and I hold hands during the Lord's Prayer, just as we reach for each other during any prayer. Sitting in the very back, next to our children's Sunday school building, gives me a different perspective. I enjoy watching my fellow parishioners worship and interact. I take a deep breath and feel grateful for our community—and to be in this marriage. I have never, not even once, had to hustle for Mike's love. His love is unconditional, and I love him back with the same fierceness. And our faith is important to us. Mike decided to be confirmed in the Episcopal Church early in our marriage.

A video camera is a few feet away, covering the service live. Having this option has been a gift for those who are unable to come to church. In addition to her own service, Mom watches ours as well. People who once lived here and were members have the chance to watch too. Covid has wreaked havoc in our lives in so many ways while forcing us to be creative. As much as I love to stay home, even if it's at someone else's house, these outdoor services bring me to community, something I also need.

After the service, folks put up chairs, cover the altar, and visit with one another. Soon, I'm ready to retreat to Lisa's. Mike and I need to prepare for our trip to Hawaii next Sunday to see Michael. As we walk back to Lisa's house, packing summer clothes and bathing suits fills my mind. Covid tests need to be scheduled seventy-two hours before arrival. I stop outside Lisa's house to hug Mike. My heart warms in his embrace.

"I love you," I say.

"I love you more," Mike says.

We say these words to each other many times a day.

Inside, I tell Lisa, "It's so cool to hear our choir and church members sing from outside your home. Of course, we were given a hard time because we were a minute or so late." I smile. "I'm going to lie down for a few minutes before lunch."

I go to the room I'm staying in and plop down on the bed. Thoughts of Mike and our short dating time float through. We spent every day together, come rain or shine, or with our hospital work.

One time, I met him at his apartment. He opened the door and I noticed again how handsome he was and how muscular his legs were. I hadn't expected to find someone like him. I wondered what it would take for me to marry someone. I thought it would mean living with him for years before saying *I do.* Instead, I felt safe with Mike from day one, and communication, faith, and patience have been the key ingredients. Even though we might not get something right, we work together until we do.

In our marriage, I'm seen and heard, and I believe I do the same for him. We don't look away from each other when we're frustrated. He doesn't have an ego that needs to be nurtured. He is sweet and thoughtful. I close my eyes and drift in my thoughts. *Thank You, Lord.*

I know Mike and I have a rare relationship and I don't take that for granted. Our first dates were so different from anything I'd experienced before. On one of them, Mike took me to the grocery store, where he picked out fresh vegetables and salmon. We then went to his apartment and he cooked dinner for us.

"You've already impressed me by your grocery selection," I said. "I grew up on canned foods and Spam."

He smiled. I looked around as he showed me his menagerie of animals. How did he manage their care and his medical residency?

"This is Sam the cat, Guy the ferret, my terrarium, and my parakeets."

Within minutes, my eyes started to itch and water and my throat felt scratchy. "Um, I'm going to have to go outside. My allergies are getting stirred up."

"I'm sorry. I've never been around someone with allergies. I thought I'd cleaned my apartment well."

I smiled. He had vacuumed but not dusted, so animal hair was everywhere.

Months later, after he moved into my house, I was struggling with asthma and needed to use my rescue inhalant. I preferred to keep this need private, but I also needed to explain the process to him.

"I need to use my inhalant," I said. "After that, I will cough for a while. I don't know how to do it with someone else around. I don't want to keep you awake."

"Please, don't worry about me. I'm not going anywhere. I love you, so I want what's best for you."

I told him I needed to take a walk. The dark night swallowed me up, as once again I felt betrayed by my body. And my anger confused me. *What's wrong with me? Why am I angry?*

When I returned home, Mike helped me untangle my emotions. "Do you think I'm going to leave you because you have asthma?"

"I don't know. I'm not used to dealing with my asthma in such an intimate way. And yes, I want to be *perfect* for you and I can't."

"You are perfect for me in every way. I don't care if you have asthma or anything else. I love *you* for who you are."

Tears rolled down my cheeks. He held me close as I gave in to coughing. I recognized that I was also emotionally safe with Mike.

He holds my heart in his gentle hands. I love him.

# CHAPTER 50

It's the beginning of spring 1980. Monday can't come soon enough. I feel sad since Andy called and that I can't get clean enough. I want to bury thoughts of him. At school and in sports, I feel free of his grime, and it doesn't take me as long to recover now that he lives in Mississippi.

I dive into my classes and keep an eye out for Coach Finnegan. Softball practices begin in a few weeks. I need the fun they will provide. My heart lurches, though, as I realize there are only two or three months left in my senior year. I want to freeze-frame this time in my life.

One day, I round the corner from the library and run smack-dab into Coach Finnegan.

"Hey, Yogi," he says. "How are you?"

I hope he can't see my heart pumping. It feels like it's going to jump out of my chest any minute. "I'm great," I answer. "How're you?"

"Wonderful. Looking forward to softball. I think we'll challenge some teams this year."

"Yeah, me too."

"You and Mary are our only seniors this year, but you make up for about four players." He laughs. "I'm expecting a lot out of you. You're a strong leader and a skilled player. Your teammates look up to you and Mary."

"We'll do our best," I reply. "I'm very excited. I'm so happy fast-pitch finally made it into the school system." I'm also a bit twitchy with my body, hoping it doesn't look like I need to go to the bathroom. I love talking with him. "I'll bring my catcher's equipment to practice and keep it here at school like I did last year."

"Thanks. Your equipment is better than the school's for sure."

The bell rings. I wish it were broken.

I sense that he wishes the bell were broken too. I hope I'm not imagining it. But his eyes look a little sad as we leave each other. A warmth comes over my body. Seeing Coach helps wash away thoughts of Andy's gunk.

There's no comparison between him and Andy. Coach Finnegan is cute, not married, and closer to my age. Andy's about twelve years older than I am, married, and, instead of being a mentor for me, he took advantage of my vulnerability. Now all I feel is shame around Andy. But Coach is so much fun to be with.

# CHAPTER 51

"Okay," Coach says. "Let's turn two."

He hits a hard grounder to third base. Sheila turns and fires to second. Then Becky, our second baseman, whips it to first. My glove pops as the ball flies home. I toss the ball under my left arm in Coach Finnegan's direction. He catches it and repeats the drill. We work well together.

"Gather in," Coach tells us.

I stand tall beside him, light as a bird and happy. Confidence flows through me from head to toe. Mary joins me.

"Defense looks great," he confirms. "The only thing we need is a pitcher. Any volunteers?"

Our former pitcher, Lori, graduated last year. We need to replace her, but it won't be me. I'm a catcher through and through. I'm needed behind the plate.

"Coach," Mary says. "I'll give it a go."

I snicker. Mary elbows me. She's the best center fielder I've ever seen. But pitching?

"Okay," he says. "Let's see what you've got, Mary. You and Yogi work together while I drill more with the defense."

Mary and I smile and find a decent spot to practice. I walk off the distance. Mary pitches short and then begins to get the ball over the plate. It's a slow pitch, but maybe it will get faster as she gets more comfortable.

"Not bad," I encourage her. "Throw harder than you think you need to."

After a little while, Coach Finnegan gathers the team again and asks Mary if she's ready to try pitching to batters. She is.

We laugh as we take our positions. After a few hitters, Mary starts to get the hang of it and her accuracy improves. I can't believe she's going to be the pitcher. We will have a lot of fun, and now I get to work closer with both Mary and Coach Finnegan. This must be what heaven feels like.

Later that week my heart falls when I receive a letter from the University of the South. They use the words *regret to inform you* and *such a good candidate* in the same paragraph. Well, if I'm such a good candidate, then why won't you accept me? Do you regret telling me? Damn the SAT. I sit still on my bed and hold my breath as I stare at the purple letterhead. I want to be a part of Sewanee. I'd hoped the letters from the clergymen would be enough, but I guess not.

I'm not smart. If I can't get into the college I want, then I'm not smart enough to be a doctor. I don't look forward to telling Dr. Curtis about this decision after he worked hard to get me into Sewanee. I think Coach Finnnegan will be disappointed too.

I feel like crying, but I don't know how Mom could have paid for such an expensive college anyway. Don mentioned helping pay for it, but I doubt he meant a university like Sewanee. Maybe I'll become a nurse instead. I'll always have a job and won't ever need to depend on anyone.

When Mom comes home, I tell her about the rejection letter.

"I'm sorry, honey."

"Me too. It was a nice rejection letter, though." I smile despite my sadness.

"What do you want to do now?"

"I'm thinking about nursing. Maybe I should look at the University of Tennessee at Chattanooga and stick around here. It'd be cheaper. And Dad/Don said he might help pay for college."

"Boy, that would be nice," Mom says.

I return to my room and pull the phone cord to my beanbag chair. Using Grandfather's business WATS line, I make the long-distance call.

After we say hello, I break the news about Sewanee. "I didn't get into the University of the South because of my SAT scores."

"Hon, if it makes you feel any better, I don't do well on standardized tests either. It wasn't easy for me to get into medical school because of my scores."

"I'm thinking of becoming a nurse and going to UTC."

"You would make a great nurse. I think that's a good plan. You won't have to deal with being on call and can work closely with patients."

His words remind me of doing therapy for Ginger's feet when she was in the hospital.

"I tell you what. I'll create a savings account in your name and start making deposits each month to help you pay for school."

I let go and feel my body being held only by my chair. I take a deep breath.

"Thank you, Dad. That would help a lot. I won't touch it except for college."

"I'll get your account started today."

"I appreciate your help. It means a lot."

"You're welcome."

"Tell Joanna hi for me."

"I will. I love you."

"I love you too."

I hang up. I think that's the first time we've said those words to each other. I push off the floor to tell Mom the good news.

Afterward, I grab my glove and ball and head to the garage. The pitch back net is light in my hands as I carry it to the backyard. The ground gives way to the spikes as I push them in as deep as I can. I throw hard at the net and am rewarded with a fast return of the ball. As I release the ball, I wonder why Don waited so long to meet us. What changed for him? I can't shake how I grew up thinking he didn't exist when all that time he'd been alive and well.

Adults don't have a clue as to how they affect children. I hope I don't forget my children and how they see the world when I become more of an adult. I'm eighteen now and am considered to be one but don't feel like it yet.

I want to be the best parent ever. I want to break the chain and do things another way. I want to marry a man who will be loyal and loving and someone I can trust all the way through. He'll be kind and gentle.

I wonder what it will take for me to find someone like that. What will make me decide to marry him? But for now, I want to surround myself with people who will love me for being me.

# CHAPTER 52

It's October 2021 and Mike and I have landed in Hawaii. Tropical winds blow through the parking garage and my dress clings to my legs. We stand side by side, agitated, wondering where Michael is. The jitters are setting in. *Where are you?* And then Mike's phone pings.

"Michael is circling all around us," Mike says. "He says that the one-way streets are confusing. I'm going to go down the road and see if I can find him." But then I spot a Kia and there is our son.

My heart pounds as I run behind his car, tears in my eyes. I can't wait to hold him. His car comes to a stop, he jumps out, and we cling to each other and warmth fills me. *Thank You.* Like a slideshow, memories flash through my mind: long, blond curls bouncing as he chases a duck, falling asleep plucking his stuffed rabbit. Or when he and other homeschool friends created a stop-action movie about soccer. At birthday parties, Michael loved watching the person of honor open their gifts. I could hold him forever.

A security man walks past us and smiles. Mike steps in to hold his son; they are alike and have always been close. Michael's first words were *da da.* At night as a three-year-old, he would stand at his bedroom window watching for his dad's truck lights, because Mike spent many late nights working in the emergency room. I picture Michael's small body sprawled asleep on the floor, his need for his father palpable. In the same way, Mike's love for his sons is strong. Even though being a rural pediatrician demanded a lot of his time, he was always present with them when he was home.

"Your dad and I haven't eaten," I say as they break apart. "Do you have time to join us for dinner before you go to work?"

"I do," he answers. "I have about an hour."

We slide our masks on and find a restaurant. We are asked to show our vaccination records and driver's licenses. The hostess looks at our information and back at us before returning them.

"Welcome to Kalo Hawaiian," she says and leads us to our table. "We serve authentic Hawaiian food."

"Thank you," I say. As she leaves, I turn to Mike and Michael. "I like how strict they are about seeing our vaccination records. It feels safer."

Michael nods. "It will be that way in any of the restaurants on Waikiki."

"In Toccoa, most people don't even wear masks."

I lean over and we hug again. I scan his handsome face without staring. Seeing him in person is so much better than on FaceTime or Zoom. Fifteen months is too long. Man, I wish Covid would go away. It interferes with everything. I also wish Matthew were here. Covid kept him from joining us. Damn Covid.

I sit back and listen to Mike and Michael talk about food and politics. I'm grateful to be here. A week will go by fast, and each day with Michael will be a treasure.

"I'll pick you up tomorrow after I wake up and get a bite to eat," Michael says. "I thought we would do a short hike to a lighthouse. I'll text you when I'm on my way."

He looks more man than child. This is the first time I've seen him this way. Like a finished puzzle, I see the whole of him now. Here in Hawaii, he has found his tribe. Michael loves this island, and his happiness is more important than my need to have him live close by. *Thank You, Lord. Thank You.*

We wave goodbye as he drives away into the night. Tomorrow begins a new day with all of us as adults. Mike and I are guests in his paradise. This switch feels so right.

I think about all the gifts I have—a relationship with God, my husband, our children, my mom, other family members, and our friends. If the pain and betrayals of my young life brought me these gifts, then they were worth it. I think about Dr. Curtis recommending that I go to therapy when I was nineteen years old. His suggestion opened a whole new world to me. I wanted to change the way I relate with others and learn about myself. I've also read all of Brené Brown's books on her grounded research around shame and emotions. I learn something new about myself with each read. I'm still a work in progress, but I believe I'm moving forward, not backward.

# CHAPTER 53

It's spring 1980. "Well, Stephanie," says Dr. Tipp, "you need all four wisdom teeth removed. Since you have asthma, I will admit you the night before the procedure."

I slump in my chair. *Asthma makes up the rules of my life.* Not only do I take medication every day for it, but I also get a shot in my arm every week, I don't roll in the grass or hang out in the woods, and now I have to be hospitalized to have my wisdom teeth removed. Shit.

"I might have an opening next Friday," I hear him say.

"I have softball games on Thursday and Friday."

"Steph," Mom says, "you need to have this done."

"Can I go to my game on Thursday?"

"Well," Dr. Tipp replies, "you'll have to ask the nursing staff when you're admitted."

"It's just that it's my senior year and I don't want to miss any games."

"I understand. They may let you leave after your lab work."

*Yes, please.*

Mom and I walk to the car. "Mom, I can't miss both games."

"Steph, I don't want you to miss any either. We'll see what happens."

Mom is one of my biggest fans.

My heart races as we head home. I feel threatened. I don't want to miss any moments away from Coach Finnegan either.

Damn wisdom teeth. Breast tumors interfered with my seventh and eighth grade basketball games and now this complication. I grip the steering wheel harder. I hate asthma. None of my friends have ever been in the hospital. Their wisdom teeth are removed in the office. This procedure will mark my fourth time being a hospital patient. Will my body ever be normal?

On Monday, I find Coach Finnegan to tell him about my upcoming surgery.

"Yogi, we'll figure this out. I think Becky can catch for us until you get back."

"I intend to play on Thursday night. I'm sure the nurses will let me leave to play."

"You need to take care of yourself. We'll miss you at Friday's game for sure."

We look into each other's eyes seconds longer than usual. I think he will miss me too, and I feel warmth down to my toes. I sense he wants to hold my hand or give me a hug. I receive it without our touching.

At home, Mom comes up with an idea. "If the nurses say no at the hospital, we'll find a way to leave anyway."

My head jerks up and I raise my eyebrows. *Is she serious? Is that legal? Will we get into trouble?*

"Okay," I say. "What's the plan?"

"Well, we can sneak out after you have your tests done. They shouldn't need you after that."

My brain starts to whirl. Walk out? Just like that? I picture myself in my robe wearing my uniform underneath.

Thursday arrives and I feel anxious about our plan. I'm admitted to a room with three other beds. A woman is in one of them.

A nurse makes quick work of getting the blood work drawn.

"Excuse me," I say, "are there any other tests to be done?"

"No."

"Well, then, may I leave for a little while to go to a softball game?"

"No. If you leave, you'll have to go through all the lab work again."

Damn. I don't want to cost Mom any more money.

Keeping an eye on the clock, Mom and I look at each other after the door closes behind the nurse.

"I'm going to put on my uniform," I say. "Of course, the game *would* be in East Brainerd." The town is fourteen miles away.

"Hurry up, honey."

I change into my uniform and zip up my robe. My glove is in the car.

"Hey, ma'am," I say to the woman across the room, "I'm going to my softball game. We'll be back as soon as possible. Would you mind not telling the nurse?"

"I won't say a word," she replies with a smile.

"Thank you."

We walk to the elevator without being seen.

I cross the lobby at Memorial Hospital to the restroom. I open a stall and shrug out of my house coat. I open my bag and pull out my cleats. My hands shake a little. I feel like I've run a race. I take a deep breath and walk out of the restroom. We shouldn't be sneaking out. I feel that familiar guilt. Mom motions me near the automatic doors. Like freed prisoners, we rush to her car and take off.

The next morning, my teeth are pulled. I vomit as soon as I wake up from the anesthesia. Yuck. I want to be like my friends. They aren't bothered by allergies, asthma, breast tumors, or having their wisdom teeth removed. Their parents are still married, and I doubt they've been molested like I have.

My thoughts take me down as Mom holds the emesis basin. Later in the day, I hear a knock on the door and Coach Finnegan peeks around it. I'm so happy to see him that my mood immediately lifts.

"I brought you the game ball. Everyone signed it for you."

"Wow, thank you. Did we win?"

"Yes. How are you feeling?"

"My stomach has been upset ever since I woke up from surgery. I hope I can go home soon."

"As soon as you can keep liquids down," Mom says, "we can leave."

"Thanks for stopping by, Coach," I say. "I'll see you at school next week."

"Okay, Yogi. See you then."

My negative thoughts vanish as fast as they came.

# CHAPTER 54

I swallow two NoDoz tablets as I steer my grandfather's van down highway I-75 South. It's the end of March 1980 and spring break—Ft. Lauderdale here we come. Six of my friends and two chaperones are sprawled out behind me. I promised Debbie's mom I would switch driving with Debbie every two hours. I hate lying, but I knew I would be fine to drive much longer than that. I'm eighteen and have been driving for a long time.

Our chaperones are already asleep. One is Karen's sister and one is Angie's. Both of the sisters are twenty years old. They are cool and promise we will have a good time. Snacks are passed over them. We choose to drive through the night so we can maximize our beach time. Excited chatter fills the back.

I love driving my grandfather's customized van. Sitting high up makes me feel older and in charge.

"How are you doing, Steph?" Debbie asks as she makes her way to the front.

"I know it's been a few hours, but I'm good," I say. I don't add that I took the NoDoz tablets and feel like running beside the van, I'm so jittery and alert. I tell Debbie to go to sleep and promise to wake her when I need to rest.

An hour later, I take a quick look in the back and nearly everyone is asleep or on their way to sleep. Most of us have played sports together for many years. Debbie and I have known each other since fourth grade. She attended St. Stephen's Country Day School too. We played basketball together from fifth grade up to this past year—minus the one year I sat out. The only barrier my friends and I have between us is that most of them are Catholic and I'm not. I've never appreciated attending required masses but not being able to participate in Holy Communion. It makes me feel less than they are.

I laugh as I think of a group of us meeting with our school priest, Father Al, last year. We gathered in the gym, our feet clattering as we climbed the stands. Father Al greeted us and remained standing on the floor.

"Father Al," I started. "We don't understand why we must attend schoolwide masses but are denied the most important part of the service—Holy Communion."

"It isn't my decision to make. As you know, the Pope makes that decision."

"But I go to church anytime I can. I even attend healing services in the summer every Wednesday. My faith means a lot to me. How's the Pope going to know if I receive communion from you?" Despite Andy and his lack of ethics, I'm happy I'm an Episcopalian. Any baptized person can receive communion in our church.

"I have taken a vow that I can't break. Only Catholics who are in good faith can receive communion."

"Well, I don't like that rule. It isn't fair for the rest of us whose churches are similar and are in *good faith* to be denied that aspect of the service."

"I hear you, Steph."

No one else added anything. What was left to say? The meeting was over in minutes. I liked Father Al and appreciated him meeting with us. Being heard felt good even if nothing changed. And in a way, I appreciated Father Al for not bending the rules he believed he must follow as a Catholic priest.

I lean up and look in the rearview mirror. It looks like everyone's asleep. The carpeted floor is filled with arms and legs. The chairs and back couch have bent heads and open mouths. My nerves feel as though they are exposed. One touch and I think I might go into a spasm. I wish I could run and get this energy out. I won't take those caffeine pills ever again.

I turn on the radio but keep the volume low. My friends trust me to keep them safe. Even though I'm the only one awake, I'm on a mission to take care of us and do not feel alone.

# CHAPTER 55

I roll over in bed to look out my sliding glass door. The lake is just beyond. Tree branches are marked with light and dark and shadows. It's the first week of November 2021 and we are living in our new house. The myriad boxes don't dampen our happiness. I can't believe Mike and I get to live in this beautiful, timber-framed home. I feel like I'm living in a dream. Despite the years, our love is growing, and we still hold hands, talk, and share ideas. And now we have built the house we fantasized about—that we built together with love.

I look at the wood patterns in the ceiling and think about the gift one of our goddaughters gave us. She and some of her friends came the day after we moved in to help unbox the kitchen, the heartbeat of our home. Creating that space helped me relax into the rest of the chaos around me. Box upon box of items we deemed necessary fill every crevice. I want to set this house up with care and thoughtfulness, the same way I feel about my inner terrain. If I need a break, I take one, and I have learned to ask for what I need. I don't like hurting anyone, but I'm now putting my needs before others. Skewed boundaries are coming into clearer focus. My responsibilities are taking care of our geriatric pups, our home, my photography business, and my writing.

I breathe in the quiet, overwhelmed by the beauty of the lake, my holy place. I can see it from three sides of our house.

Unbelievable. A gaggle of geese lands near our dock. I stop my work to watch them swim. Their honking sounds remind me of when we lived on the lake years earlier. I've missed their cries.

I'm grateful Mike has had his Covid booster. I'll get mine as soon as I'm allowed. So much has changed for me from March 2020 until now. We wear our masks everywhere we go, and I imagine this protocol will be the new norm for years to come. Slowing down and spending more time alone opens my heart. I notice my survival instinct taking a backseat. God's presence is easier to recall. As I begin lining another set of drawers, I picture a spinning wheel with a mouse on it. Memories of my running from one event to another and feeling utter exhaustion appall me. I hope I don't ever jump back on the wheel. I don't grieve that part of my life. Sometimes I pray the Serenity Prayer more than once a day:

*God, grant me the serenity to accept the things I cannot change, the courage to change the things I can, and the wisdom to know the difference. Amen.*

*Thank You, God.*

When Mike gets home he informs me that three of his patients tested positive for Covid. So, the virus continues. My mother remarked today that all she and her husband and friends do is go to doctors' appointments. I tell Mike, "Mom also said that when they're not going to doctors, they're going to funerals. I told her that going to see the doctors kept them from being the ones the funerals are for. She laughed."

Mike smiles. "You two are so silly."

"I know. You should've been with us a few years ago when she broke her neck, back, and ribs. As awful as the situation was, Mom and I were able to laugh. We made that time fun."

# CHAPTER 56

It's April 1980. The creek water feels cool. I squat at its edge and scoop up sediment. My pan fills with small rocks and dirt. I look over at Mary.

"See anything?" I ask her.

"Not yet."

"I love that we get to go camping for our science club," I say. "I don't care if I find any gold or not."

Mary's brows furrow as she digs into the creek. I sit back on my heels and look around. Coach Finnegan is one of our chaperones. Being with him outside school is my gold. I see him heading our way, but he stops to investigate a student's pan. He shakes it for a minute and looks at it. Coach Finnegan smiles and shakes his head and returns the pan. I rub my hands together.

"Find any gold yet?" he asks us.

"Not yet, but we aren't giving up."

Mary's boyfriend, Daniel, takes a break and talks with Coach. A burst of energy comes over me and I grab my pan and dig into the chilly water again. After an hour, we leave for our campground. My friends pile into my grandfather's van and I drive behind the others. We are in Franklin, North Carolina, a pretty town.

The campground is full of trees and shade. I park the van on a flat surface close to the other vehicles and we pile out and set up tents. The smell of pine washes over me. I may sleep inside Grandfather's van, but I help the others set up their tents. I still don't sleep well around other people. After our makeshift meal over the fire, a group of us entice Coach Finnegan into the van to play cards. I pull him by his arm and lead him. He laughs.

Poker seems to be the top choice for card games. We arrange ourselves on the back couch, captains' chairs, and the front seats, with Coach Finnegan and me taking over the driver and passenger seats. Our laughter swells inside the carpeted vehicle. Kenny Rogers' song "The Gambler" comes on the radio. All of us sing it at the top of our lungs and Coach Finnegan joins in. We hold each other's eyes while we sing and laugh.

The evening comes to an end sooner than I want. I could play cards with Coach and my friends all night. I join my girlfriends in a tent and lie awake. I replay tonight and think of Coach and how much fun we had. *I will never forget this evening.*

Back in Chattanooga, Dr. Curtis, my priest, urges me to attend the Episcopal youth weekend called Happening. I didn't know our church had a spiritual weekend for teenagers. The previous year, I attended the Catholic version called Search. No one else from our youth group is going. I hem and haw for a while but agree to attend.

The conference is in Monteagle, a few miles from Sewanee. I drive myself up and focus on my last time here with my volleyball team; any thoughts of Andy are crowded out. According to Dr. Curtis, there will be youth from all over Tennessee, I just won't know any of them. The conference center is white with tile roofing and wide arches, like Don and Joanna's Las Vegas house. I swallow and walk towards it. *I can do this.* If I can speak in front of adults at a sports banquet as I did last week, I should be able to meet people my own age.

After registration we are given the names of our family groups and disappear to separate meeting rooms. Our group sits in a circle. I glance at my peers and look down at the old, red carpet. There are no adults with us. One of the youths speaks up and introduces himself. He has white skin, long black hair, and blue eyes. A bandanna wraps around his left hand and wrist. He seems cool and a bit cocky.

"I'm Will Kidd," he says. "I'm seventeen and I'm from Oak Ridge, Tennessee. Let's go around the circle and introduce ourselves and say where we're from."

The girl to his left introduces herself and we make it all the way back to him. Will begins to talk about his faith and what he hopes to get out of the weekend. A few others also share, but I skip this part. I feel strong in my faith and don't feel the need to talk about it to people I don't know. I'd rather remain quiet.

A bell chimes in the distance.

"I guess it's time for us to meet with everyone else," Will says.

We follow him out and return to the big gathering room. I look out the window and see a rope hanging where the bell must be. We have Holy Eucharist and then go to the dining hall for some hamburgers and fries. I sit next to a few people from our small group. The name tags help me learn who they are. I take a deep breath. *It's cool to be with other Episcopal youth.*

After breakfast the next day, we break into our family groups. The dining hall and hallways begin to feel familiar. I smile at my peers and find myself looking at Will. He points to paper, crayons, pens, and envelopes.

"Let's write down our first impressions of each other," he says. "No one will see these. Just you. And then you can use the envelopes to seal them up."

I hesitate. What's the point of this exercise? I look around and see the others finding places in the room to write. I guess I'll do it.

The next morning, after our family group time, we watch a powerful video about Jesus and his crucifixion. I don't like seeing Him crucified; it's so barbaric. I prefer to think of His resurrection and His life before and after the crucifixion. After the video, we have free time outside to play games. I really need to move my body.

After dinner, we're blindfolded and led somewhere. When we stop, I can tell we are in a building or room of sorts. The sound is muffled.

"Okay," an adult leader says. "Take off your blindfolds."

I rip mine off. We are in a room decorated for a party. All of a sudden, loud music erupts from the stereo. A long table holds snacks and punch. How cool is this? I join in the dancing. A part of me still holds back, but I'm having a good time. I wish I weren't so cautious with my feelings or trust. I notice other teenagers laughing and being crazy. I don't know how to let loose like that.

The song "Celebrate" comes on. *I love this song.* When I see everyone getting in a line, I join in and follow the group's steps. Feeling like a part of the group is so great. I jump up and down and clap. I wipe sweat from my forehead. I want the song to never end.

After an hour or so, we are given bags with our names on them and return to our family groups. Will shares a personal story and I admit to myself that he has a way with words. I can see him becoming a priest when he gets older. He's cute and charismatic, too. As I listen, I feel closer to him and think I may have misjudged him. When he finishes, we hug him and each other and then open our bags.

I pull out a Happening #5 T-shirt, along with handmade necklaces and a lot of letters. I read each one, filled with love. I hear a few people crying. Will has written me a letter, too. I knew he was a leader of some sort, but he's been acting like he's one of us while guiding us through the activities. I love all the notes—some from people I know and some from others I just met. What a night.

After Holy Eucharist and breakfast the next day, we return to our family's room. We talk about last night and our *caritas* gifts. I'm tired but happy. I will miss Will and some of the other teenagers.

"I guess you've figured out I'm our group's leader," Will says.

We nod our heads and laugh.

"Would any of you be willing to share your first impressions?" he asks.

My stomach drops. I'm not going to share, because I didn't write the nicest things about Will. I like him now, but I wasn't sure of him in the beginning. A few offer to read theirs. Of course, they have positive things to say. Will looks at me and challenges me to share. My mouth goes dry and my hands sweat.

"Um," I stammer. "My first impressions were off. I don't want to read mine."

"Don't worry," he says. "I'll be fine."

No. No. No. I don't want to hurt him. I don't want to lose him as my friend. I can't tell him the truth.

"I promise your words won't hurt me," he reassures me. "We are friends and will remain so."

Is he reading my mind?

I feel my face flush as I read my first impressions of him out loud. "Will seems full of himself. He's cocky and self-assured. He knows he's cute . . ."

I leave nothing out. I can't believe I'm saying these things out loud. My stomach clenches. As I finish reading, I glance up at him, but I find only love in his eyes.

"I'm sorry," I say. "I made a hasty decision about you. It makes me wonder how many other people I may do this to."

"Steph," he says, "it's okay. The exercise is meant for us to recognize how most of us do just that on a regular basis. Thank you for sharing."

We come in for a group hug. My underarms feel prickly; I hope I don't smell. I feel like I have been run through a wringer. I press hard against him but still feel terrible. What a powerful lesson to learn.

I head down the mountain and know I'll be back. I'll try to be on the celebration staff next time. I'm not sure I feel up to being a family group leader like Will. That takes a lot of guts. *Thank you, Dr. Curtis, for pushing me into this gathering.*

# CHAPTER 57

"Smile," Mom says as she raises her camera.

It's prom night and I'm going with Bryan, a friend of my brother's, but I'm not interested in him. All I want to do is see Coach, who promised to dance with me.

"Okay," I say. "It's time for us to leave."

"I'll see you in a little while," she replies.

My yellow-flowered corsage hangs on my thin, blue dress. The hem reaches the floor. I feel pretty. My date, Bryan, who's at least six feet tall, takes my arm and leads me to his muscle car, his face flushed. Bryan's been wanting to go on a date with me for a while. I don't like using him, so I will be as nice as I can.

After closing the door for me, Bryan climbs into the car. I see him as a bit of a redneck, like Brandon. He's wearing an open shirt and jacket and no tie. He's shy, so our conversation on the way to the dance is sparse. We pull up in front of the Chester Frost Park Pavilion and Bryan opens my door and helps me out. Not like I need any help getting out—I can't wait to see Coach.

Inside, I make a beeline for my friends. Mary looks beautiful. All my friends do. I introduce my date to everyone. Everything is decorated in green and gold. I see various teachers standing around the periphery while I scan the room for

Coach, but I don't find him. My heart drops a little. I see Mom and some other parents slip through the door.

Music floods the room. We dance with each other and our dates. I keep a smile on my face while I watch the door. *Please come. I want one dance with you.* As if by magic, Coach Finnegan walks inside. He's smiling so big, I can see his dimples from the dance floor. He joins some of the other teachers and leans against the wall. I position myself so I can see him. Even with the dim lights, I see him looking at me and I smile.

A little while later, I'm breaking out in a sweat from all the dancing. Bryan and I go to the refreshment table and get some punch. I guzzle it down and slip over to where Coach stands.

"Are we going to dance?"

"Of course. As soon as there's a slower song. I'm not a great dancer."

I feel my breath catch and my palms sweat. I don't know why I thought he'd change his mind.

"All right, then," I say. "As soon as there's a slow song, you're up."

His eyes pierce mine. For a second, I see sadness. But then he breaks into a smile. I wonder if he's feeling what I'm feeling. As seniors, our classes ended several weeks before the rest of the school. I stayed in my Math IV class so I could still see him. Is he dreading my leaving too?

It's almost time to declare the prom king and queen. I'm not on the ballot, but several of my friends are. Bryan and I walk over to Mom. She asks us if we're having fun.

I nod—*especially now that Coach Finnegan is here and we have a dance coming up.*

The king and queen are announced. We rush our friend as she's being crowned. I'm so happy for her. Loud cheers fill the room as a special dance takes place for the king and queen. We clap as the couple exits the floor. My fingers cross in hopes the next song will be a slow one.

I hear Leo Sayer's "When I Need You" come on. I let Bryan know I will be dancing with one of my teachers, and just like that I find myself floating to Coach. He meets me near the dance floor. I see Mom over my shoulder, but I can't read her expression. I feel exposed. I've never been one to hide my feelings; if I'm mad at someone, they know. Mom may or may not know how I feel about Coach or how I've had a crush on him for the past two years. I dismiss these thoughts and enjoy being in his arms. We are a good physical fit.

I lean into him as he pulls me closer, our bodies like magnets. His heart beats fast. Is he nervous? My hand fits his just right. He smells clean and of shampoo. I drop my head on his shoulder and close my eyes. I hope no one is paying attention to us. I don't want Leo to stop singing. I long to be held this way by Coach forever.

As the song comes to an end and we pull apart, I see the sadness return again in his eyes. I want to disappear and cry my heart out. Is this dance our last time together? It feels like my life is over. Will I ever see him again? I'm eighteen and he's twenty-five; I'll be graduating this month. How do these things work? Does he feel the way I do? Will I ever find out? What am I going to do?

I plaster a smile on my face for the rest of the night.

# CHAPTER 58

It's the first day of November 2021. Mountains surround the small town, so clouds weave in and out of the sun. I find the new address and wait in my car as instructed. I can't believe it's been over a year since I've seen Brooke in person. During our time of teletherapy, she moved into two new offices, one in another state but not too far away and one down the street from her former office.

I see her through the window as she walks onto the porch. She waves at me and motions me inside. I slip my mask on. It's weird seeing her in a mask, but I can tell she's smiling. I'm happy to see her in person too.

She welcomes me in and introduces me to a woman sitting behind a desk. We continue to the back where her new office is. The space is larger and airier than her last one. Brooke sits at her desk while I move to the opposite side and sit on a couch. She removes her mask. I do the same.

"I like your new office, but where's your Winnie-the-Pooh picture?"

"It's still in my old place. None of the furniture here is mine. I share this office with another person."

We begin by talking about how writing my memoir has helped put my past in a new light and how I've enjoyed having a longtime acquaintance edit the memoir, especially by taking some of the embarrassment out of the parts that are sexual in nature. And how the more I work on the memoir, the easier the remembering gets.

Brooke smiles at me and takes a sip from her coffee cup.

"I had a dream last week that I think made me feel powerful."

"Tell me about it."

"I'm at an Episcopal convention and Andy is there too. I've had a similar dream several times while writing about my past. I feel angry, like *why is he here*? This time, I find myself standing in a pulpit. He is in another pulpit, diagonal from me and at some distance—not in a lofty one where he would be looking down but at an equal height. He starts talking about women and their *place*. I'm furious. *He has no right to talk about women!* I interrupt him from across the room. I begin telling all the people on the floor—priests, bishops, and the other Episcopalians—what he did to me."

Brooke's eyes sparkle. "I love that you placed yourself and Andy on the same level. And you were *both* standing in pulpits."

"I know. I recognize the power of my position in the dream—I'm now on equal footing. After I speak, the leaders in the room gravitate to me and help me down. I look over and see the security people pull Andy down and begin to take him away. I answer questions and begin to tell my story. I felt so empowered."

"Your dream says a lot about where you are."

"I think so too. When I woke up, I felt a shift in me. I knew that dream said a lot about where I am in my healing. It's the first one where my voice was heard and acted upon in regard to Andy. I was a victim then, but not now."

Brooke smiles and nods. We sit in silence until an image pops in my head.

"I once told you about how I used to find myself sitting on the floor and shaking and feeling cold after conversations with my birth father. I thought I was weak, but you identified my reaction as post-traumatic stress disorder. It started after Dad/ Don told me he could live without me. He had done it once and he could do it again."

"Yes, I remember."

"The repetition of writing and going over it line by line with my editor makes all these secrets easier to bear."

We then discuss how often, or not, I want to meet with her. "I would like to keep seeing you until I finish my book. I have more tough stuff to write about. How about we meet once a month for now?"

"That sounds good. Let's make your next appointment now."

I smile. "Being able to talk things through with you has been such a gift. I appreciate your listening and expertise, Brooke. Thank you."

"It is my pleasure. See you next month."

We fist-bump and I walk to my car. I rest my hands on the steering wheel and breathe in gratefulness. I'm proud of my work. All these years of reading books, taking classes, and going to therapy have paid off. Writing is such a powerful tool. The one that digs the deepest. *Thank You, God.*

# CHAPTER 59

It's the week after graduation. I feel miserable, like a part of me is missing. I wipe my eyes and roll onto my stomach. I'm able to cry again. It took my deep-felt love for Coach Finnegan to release my tears. I love him and don't know how I'll go on without seeing him. How can I fix this? I don't want to do anything but see Coach. But does he feel the same way? Maybe it doesn't matter. I need to tell him how I feel. Maybe he can help me deal with these feelings.

My palms sweat as I go to the kitchen for the phone book. I don't even know if he's in the directory. I run my finger down the Fs and find him. My chest tightens. I write down his number and go to my room and shut the door. No one's home, but I need to feel safe. Bread's "Baby I'm-a Want You" comes on the radio. I love their music.

I pick up my phone and dial Coach's number. My hand shakes. *I can't do this.* He picks up right before I hang up.

"Hello?"

"Uh," I say. "Hi, Coach. It's Stephanie."

"Hey, Stephanie. How are you?"

His voice sounds different over the phone.

"I'm good. How're you?"

"Doing well. Taking it easy."

"I was wondering if we could meet somewhere. I need to talk with you. I have a problem I'm hoping you can help me with."

"Sure. Can you meet me outside of Point Park on Lookout Mountain?"

My heart pounds. He's willing to meet me. "I can."

"How 'bout we meet around 4:00? There are benches outside the park, and there should be spaces available for parking at that time."

"Great. I'll see you then."

I place my phone on the banana-shaped holder and scream. I feel like I'm floating. What will I wear? Maybe my cutoff jean shorts and a T-shirt. I pace around the house then go outside to shoot some hoops until it's time to leave. The drive will take forty minutes or so. Dad/Tom pays for my gas and I have let go of worrying about the cost.

I make the drive and find a parking place right away. I hop out of the van. As soon as I look up, I see Coach walking toward me, his hands in his pockets. He's so cute. A breeze blows hair in my eyes and my mouth goes dry. What am I going to say? What am I doing here?

"Hey, Yogi."

"Hey, Coach. Thanks for meeting me."

"Of course. I hope I can help. What's going on?"

We sit down on one of the concrete benches. I slip my hands underneath me and swing my legs. My body is so tense that it's hard to breathe. I look around the tree-lined street and nearby houses.

"I don't know if I can say what I need to say."

"Just say it. It's all right."

I seem to lose control of myself. My body won't do what it's supposed to do. I feel woozy and words are lost to me. Now that he's beside me, I can't seem to speak.

"Would it help if I stood behind you?" he asks. "You could ask what you need to while facing forward. Pretend I'm not here."

I feel silly and immature while he stands behind me and I remain sitting on the bench. But I don't want to take up his time, so I need to spit it out.

"I have a problem," I say. "I'm in love with you and I don't know what to do about it."

I feel like mush. Did I really say that out loud? I sense him getting closer and his head comes into view.

"I have the same problem," he says. "I feel the same way about you."

An electric shock goes through me. *No way.* Coach gives me his hand to help me up and then I feel his arms go around me, pulling me into him. His heart is hammering just like mine. I hug him with all I have. I can't believe this. I'm so happy. We pull away long enough to kiss. I'm on fire. His kiss is soft and hungry. I'm not aware of anything but him and his lips. We stop long enough to sit back down on the hard bench.

The wind picks up. I lean into him while we hold hands. He tells me to call him by his first name, Gary.

"Where do we go from here?" I ask.

"I think it would be best if we kept our relationship private for now. People might not understand."

"I'm eighteen and a graduate, but I understand."

My heart feels full of tears, happy ones. For the first time this year, life feels right. My worries about losing him are over. I'm proud of myself for calling him and letting him know how I feel. I want to shout out my love for him and his for me, but I can keep our relationship quiet. Whatever he needs for us to be together.

"I start a summer job next week," he says. "Are you available next Friday night?"

"I am. I'm working first shift this summer as a nursing assistant at East Ridge Hospital, so I'll be free every afternoon after three."

"Great. I'll see you next week, Stephanie."

We wrap ourselves around each other and kiss before leaving. I feel like I'm in a fairy tale. I can't stop smiling as I drive down the mountain. I sure wish I could share this news with Mary and my other friends. They wouldn't believe it. Yet my relationship with Coach Finnegan is more important than my need to tell them. I can't wait until Friday.

On Friday, Gary drives me through his childhood neighborhood. He talks about his dad being a contractor and then shows me streets that are named after him and his brothers. When he isn't changing gears, we hold hands.

"It's crazy that we both lived in East Brainerd and ended up at the same high school," I say.

Gary laughs and smiles. The windows are down. We talk over the radio music.

I like the way I feel with him. I hope we have many more days together like this one.

The next week, Gary invites me to spend the night. I'm excited and a little scared. I'm not ready for sex yet. Before I leave, I find Mom to tell her I won't be home that night. I know if I don't tell her where I am, she'll panic.

"Where will you be?"

"I'm going to stay over at Gary's."

"No, you aren't."

"Mom, nothing is going to happen. I promise. Please, this night is important to me."

"How old is he?"

"Twenty-five."

"Stephanie, you might not be thinking about sex, but I bet he is."

"I won't do anything but sleep beside him. I love him, Mom."

"I want his phone number."

"Why?"

"I want to know that you're okay."

"I'll give you his number, but please don't call."

Mom frowns. I bet she's going to call her boyfriend as soon as I leave. Gee whiz.

I drive up Lookout Mountain to Gary's apartment and he greets me at the door. My heart is beating as fast as a hummingbird's wings. I step through the doorway and into his arms. We kiss and float around the apartment, laughing at each other. I'm so glad his roommate is gone.

"Are you hungry?' he asks.

"Yes."

"I'm not much of a cook. Will grilled cheese sandwiches work?"

"I love grilled cheese sandwiches."

I study the small kitchen while he makes our sandwiches. The clock reads 7:00. If our relationship continues like it is, I wonder if I'll move in with him here.

He hands me my sandwich on a plate. "Here you go."

I love it when he smiles. He has a strong, broad jaw so his dimples soften his face. "Thank you. It smells good."

We sit at an old white kitchen table that only has room for two. As we eat, our feet find each other under the little table. Gary and I seem to be a perfect match. He and I have so much in common and are about the same height. I'm so glad I called him and confessed my feelings for him and that he was brave enough to be truthful with me. I'm so happy.

When we're done eating, he asks if I want to watch TV.

"Sure."

"How about *The Tim Conway Show?*"

"He's so funny. I love watching him."

We snuggle on a couch and laugh as we watch. After the show, we decide it's time for bed.

I'm surprised at how calm I feel now that the time has come to sleep together. I don't think Gary will expect me to do something I'm not comfortable with. His full-size bed is tucked in between two walls. He's gentle and has a big smile on.

"Steph, we'll just snuggle tonight. Is that all right?"

I smile back. My heart warms at his understanding. "That would be great," I answer.

He takes off his shirt and pants and climbs in. I feel so lucky as I change into my pajamas in the bathroom.

After I scoot into bed next to him, we wrap our arms around each other. I ask him if I may feel his chest and face.

"Of course."

I slide my right hand along his skin. He feels perfect. I relax beside him and feel safe. We fall asleep in each other's arms.

*Ring. Ring. Ring.*

Gary picks up the phone. It's late in the night. "Hello," I hear him say and then, "Sure. She's right here."

My eyes go wide. It must be my mom, ruining a lovely night. Gary hands me the phone.

"Hello."

"Steph, are you all right?" Mom says.

"Yes. We were asleep."

My heart hammers inside my chest. The noise scared me and now I feel angry at my mom for interrupting my night with Gary.

"Okay. I just wanted to check on you."

"I'm fine. I'll talk with you tomorrow."

"I'm sorry for the interruption," I say to Gary as I hand the phone back to him.

"It's okay," Gary says. "Come here."

I lie down beside him. We kiss and then fall back asleep. I love this man.

# CHAPTER 60

It's July 1980. I slip into Gary's car. We've had a month and a half together. He's excited to show me the University of the South and I'm thrilled we won't have to hide. This past month has been both wonderful and frustrating. Several times when we've gone to his place, he's pushed my head down as we pass students' hangouts. I feel humiliated when he does that. It didn't bother me the first few times, but now it does. I was about to say something to him, but then he suggested we go somewhere we could be free of prying eyes.

With the windows down, I rest my arm outside the car. We listen to the radio and sing at the top of our lungs. He points to an old church off the highway and tells me its history. As we climb Monteagle Mountain, Gary gears down. Tractor trailers stay in the right lane as they strain to pull themselves up.

After lunch and swimming in Lake Cheston, we go on a hike. I'm so happy. Gary and I need to make this area our new date place. All we do is spend time at his house, and I'm ready for more. I don't want to think too much about our hiding and what that might mean. He's not that much older. We shouldn't have to hide much longer.

It turns out Gary has other ideas. "Hey, Steph. Come sit with me."

A creek runs beside the trail, and I join him on a rock.

"I need to talk with you," he starts.

My antenna goes up. Something seems to be wrong. He looks serious.

"Football practice starts up soon."

"Uh huh."

"And I'm going to be busy with practice and work."

"Okay, we can work around your schedule. I don't start nursing school until September."

"Well, I think it would be best if we had some distance."

I feel like I've been hit in the chest. What's going on? I know his roommate doesn't like Gary dating me. Did he put pressure on him? Where's this change coming from?

I jump up off the rock and stare down at him. Pain and panic set in.

"Please don't look at me like that." His eyes fill with tears. "I don't want to hurt you."

A little late for that. "Are you breaking up with me? We've just had a wonderful day together. I don't understand."

"I know. I care about you. But thinking about football practice brings me back to teaching and worrying about our relationship."

"So you need space?"

"I think so."

My mouth goes dry. I feel anger welling up. I can't believe him. Why did he bring me up here? To break things off? We had fun. We love each other. I don't understand.

We leave immediately. On the drive back to Chattanooga, I don't look at him or talk to him. I'm devastated, angry, and sad, and feel like I've been kicked in the guts. My heart feels like it's dropped into my belly. When I get home, I throw myself on my bed and sob. It seems like I'm not meant to be happy for any length of time; I get a taste of happiness and then it disappears. Why does this always happen to me? Life sucks. It's better to not love others. Every time I do, I get hurt.

I roll around the bed and then prop myself on my elbows. I blow my nose only to have more tears roll down my face. What am I going to do? I'll be stuck in Chattanooga—with him in reach but not available. What can I do to give him space?

An idea pops into my head. *Move to Las Vegas. Stay with your dad while you give Gary space.* Why not? Even if the bottom line for me is not seeing Gary, I can spend some time with my dad. Brilliant.

I pick up the phone and call Dad/Don. He picks up after the fourth ring.

"Hey, Dad," I say. "I was thinking. What if I took a semester off from college to live with you and Joanna? We could get to know each other better."

"Hum. Let me talk it over with Joanna and get back to you."

"Okay, thanks."

"You should touch base with UTC first, though, to make sure it won't be a problem."

"I will."

We hang up and I go to the kitchen for the directory. I call the School of Nursing and speak with one of the professors. I learn I will spend an extra year in college if I take the first semester off. The nursing program starts in the second semester, and I won't have enough hours to get in. Oh well. It'll be worth it if I can get Gary back.

I call Mom at work to tell her about my idea. "I'm thinking of taking the first semester off and living with Dad and Joanna. It seems like a good time to get to know him better. Is that okay with you?"

"What about school?"

"I'll start when I get back. Don't worry, I *will* go to college. Starting late will delay my getting into the nursing program, but that's all right. Maybe I can double major." I reassure her again. "I'll make sure I'm not ever dependent on anyone else. I'll always have a job."

"What's your dad say?"

"He's going to get back to me after he talks with Joanna."

"Okay. See you at home."

Later that night, Dad calls back and says I can come. I'm not sure what it will be like living with my birth father, but I'm excited to be with Joanna. I should be able to get through a few months, and if it's distance Gary needs, then it's distance he'll get. Maybe, just maybe, he'll feel better about us when I get back and we can pick up where we left off. I love him and won't let him go.

# CHAPTER 61

I look out my office window. The blue water and cloudy skies stare back. It's just after Christmas 2021, and we've been in our new lake house for close to a month. I take a big breath and am rewarded with the smell of paint and wood.

I hear steps on the stairs. Mike walks into my office and sits in his grandfather's cane chair next to my desk. "What're you thinking about?" he asks.

"How I can't wait for this summer and jumping in the lake."

He nods and puts his hand on my shoulder. "I'm going to go work in the yard now." He stands up to walk downstairs and out the front door.

I go over to the window facing the lake, my hands resting on the strong wood. A few fishermen go buzzing by. I can't believe where my life is today, so loved and supported. And I'm able to give love and support with little effort—unlike the times when I was in survival mode. More and more I treat myself like I do my friends.

Mike reminds me of his love daily with his colored notes. I look out the window at him working in the yard. I'm so grateful to be the luckiest girl in the world. *Thank You, Lord.*

My cell phone rings, breaking my reverie. "Hey, Mom."

"Hey, hon. Can you help me with ordering food for next week? You'd think I would figure this thing out."

I direct her how to use FaceTime so I can guide her. I hope she lives to see one hundred.

When we're done, I tell her, "You know, I'm so thankful Don didn't raise me."

"Oh, Lord. Me too."

I can't picture Don playing with Brandon and me the way Tom did. Our stepfather was just who we needed. He treated us like we were his own children.

# CHAPTER 62

It's the end of July 1980. I arrive in Las Vegas with a broken heart. I sit on Michelle's old bed and prop my feet on my blue suitcase on the floor—my back to the door. She married her boyfriend and lives in North Carolina now. The past few months rush through me and I begin to cry like my life is over. Joanna hears me and enters the room and sits beside me.

"What's the matter?" she asks.

"I can't believe I put myself so far away from the guy I love."

I tell her about Gary and our relationship. She's the first one I've told the whole story. I hinted to Barney and Brenda about Gary before I left Chattanooga, but that was it.

"He said he would write and call me," I tell Joanna. "That will help a lot. And I've never been away from home as long as I will be on this trip."

Joanna rubs my back while she listens. Every now and then she makes soothing noises. I lean into her and release all the pent-up feelings I've tucked away.

"I'm not sure I like this guy," she says.

"He was great until he took me to Sewanee and told me he needed space."

Joanna has a way to make me laugh and she somehow has me tickled. She sits with me until my tears dry.

A few weeks later, Dad asks me a strange question. "You'd like to wash my van, wouldn't you?"

"I can't do it tonight," I say. "I'm working with the youth group at the Episcopal church I've been attending. But I can do it tomorrow."

He doesn't say anything, but I'm proud of myself for creating a community the first week here. I joined a coed volleyball team too.

The next morning, I see Don when I come out to make my breakfast. "Hey Dad."

Don doesn't respond to me. He thumbs through the mail, then gathers his keys and walks out.

What's the matter with him?

A few minutes later, Joanna comes down the hall with rollers in her hair. Maybe she knows what's up. "Dad just left without speaking to me. Do you know why?"

"Oh, he gets something up his craw and does that. He mentioned something about asking you to wash the van and you didn't do it."

"I told him I would be happy to wash it today. I had a youth group meeting last night." Joanna shrugs.

He's a strange man. I go outside and wash the van. When he returns hours later, I tell him, "Hey, Dad. I washed your van today." No response.

The next morning, I hear Joanna calling me. "He's gone," she says.

I poke my head out the door and join her in the den. "Does he do this to you too?"

"I know how to handle him. He isn't used to anyone standing up to him."

A few hours later, we are laughing about something Joanna's said when we hear Don's car pull in. I stand up. "I'll see you later," I say.

Now, as soon as he comes home from work, I disappear to my room. Whenever Dad leaves the house, Joanna and I do ceramics or run errands together. I love this time with her.

Two weeks later, out of the blue, Dad calls me from work. "I'm on my way to pick you up," he says. "Grab your squash racquet and be waiting out front for me."

I hang up. My jaw is on the ground. I find Joanna. "Dad just called. He's invited me to play squash with him. I can't do that. He hasn't apologized for the way he's treated me."

"Oh, no. You must get ready. This is his way of apologizing."

"I don't understand."

"He's apologizing by calling you and inviting you to play squash. Go get ready."

I wait outside, my squash racket solid in my hand. I don't know what to expect. Two weeks without acknowledging my existence is tough to swallow and let go of. I've lived like an outsider, like I don't belong here, since he stopped acknowledging my existence. He has hurt me. He doesn't get to act like nothing is wrong, but I don't know how to play his game. It goes against my nature. He has been mean to me. A jerk.

Dad pulls in. His hair is disheveled from having the convertible's top down. I slip in the passenger seat and lean close to the door.

As we drive, my ponytail whips in the wind. I look away from him. Don owes me an apology. I washed his damn van the next day, and he failed to tell me that I had to meet his demands or else. Anger burns below the surface.

He parks outside the Sporting House. "I'll meet you on the court in five minutes," he says.

I nod my head and walk down the hall, past the bar and basketball court, and through the door to the squash court.

I beat the ball with my racquet, imagining it's him. Where did he learn how to be an asshole? I grip my racquet and whack the ball hard against the walls over and over. This game bonded us my last time here. I don't see that happening today.

Dad's shoes squeak as he enters the court and I toss him the hot ball. He tosses it back to me for me to start the serve.

*Tha-whack* sounds reverberate off the walls. I put everything I have into my hits and strategy. I'm playing my best game yet and I speak with my actions. Dad stops the game in the middle of a point and slams his racket against the wall. It breaks on impact.

"You wish this ball was my head, don't you?" he yells at me.

My eyes widen at his abruptness. I'm not sure if I'm supposed to respond. In my mind, I answer back, *why yes, I do,* but I don't say anything out loud.

We return home in a blur. I wonder how long he will refuse to speak to me this time.

At home, I catch Joanna's eyes looking at me and I drop my face. We have a complete conversation without words. I stay in my room until Joanna calls me to supper after Dad leaves for his rounds at the hospital.

I tell Joanna what happened on the court. "I can't believe he threw his racket. There's no way I'd throw mine. I keep the price tag on the handle so I don't forget how much it cost. And I don't act like a child."

"Like I said the other day, your dad is not used to anyone standing up to him. Everyone gives in to him." She smiles. "You're as stubborn as he is."

I don't know how else to be, but I don't want to be like him.

A few weeks later, I'm sitting at a table by the pool when Dad comes home. I glance up at him quickly as he comes through the garage, but I can tell he's angry.

He slams down his briefcase. "You think I'm a son of a bitch, don't you!"

I try to look cool while my heart hammers in my chest. I hold my breath.

He rips off his sunglasses. "Either you love me or you hate me."

I stare at him. He's not a tall man, but he is towering over me with the sun behind his head. I keep still.

"I'll put you on the next plane to Atlanta if that's what you want."

"I'm here until November," I say. "If you put me on a plane, it's because you want me to leave."

He stares at me. I stare back with a lift to my chin. I don't like him putting words in my mouth.

Dad snatches his briefcase and heads inside.

Now what? Do I stay out here until Joanna lets me know it's safe to come inside? I'll wait at least until my heart settles down. I let out a deep breath, feeling his rejection to my bones. I hurt and feel abandoned all over again.

After a while, Dad leaves and Joanna joins me outside. "Wow," she says. "You really stood up to him. He doesn't know what to do with that."

"Is he sending me away?"

"He didn't say a word about it when he came in. I was in the den when I saw him throw down his briefcase. Geez."

"He scared me to death when he did that. I could tell he was mad by the way he came out of the garage. I didn't expect him to do that, though."

"No, neither did I."

I shake my head. "I can't cave. It feels like losing. I'm so glad my other dad raised me. If I learn nothing else from this time here, I know that much."

This time I *know* I didn't do anything wrong—unlike my past when I took on feelings of shame and guilt. This man, my birth father, didn't even come out and ask me to wash his car. He just assumed he could boss me around.

I was honest with him. My mistake was in not understanding his way of communication: Cow down and cater to him and things will be smooth. Plus, he abandoned me when I was an infant. He should be apologizing to me instead of yelling at me. I don't like or trust him. I can't think of one good thing to say about him.

So far Gary hasn't answered any of my letters. I decide to call him. I ask him why he hasn't written.

"I've been busy with football and teaching."

I don't know why, but I don't buy this excuse. "Are practices and school going well?"

"Yes."

He doesn't ask me anything and sounds like a robot.

As I hang up the phone, I hurt all over. I feel disposable by both him and Don. What have I done to deserve their neglect? I opened my heart to Gary and he dropped it. With Don, I'm trying to get to know him and he ignores me. What do I do that pushes people away?

# CHAPTER 63

It's November of 1980 when I return home to Chattanooga. Right away, I go to Gary's new place. I called him several times from Las Vegas and felt disregarded. I'm still hurt, but anger acts as my disguise. I want to know what's going on.

I pull into the short driveway and knock on his door. He opens it, we look at each other, and then he pulls me into a hug. He invites me inside.

I plop down on his couch while he eases into a recliner. He begins to clean his fingernails. The room is small but feels large. He seems so far away.

"Gary, what's going on? Why didn't you call me and write me like you said you would?"

"I've been busy. I'm teaching more classes this year and with football . . ."

I feel my heart thumping in my chest. I'd been singing Bread's "It Don't Matter to Me" on my way here. But it *does* matter to me.

I feel like an intruder. He's not saying anything—just playing with his fingernails like they're the most important thing in the world.

I swallow down tears. I feel the same pain now that I felt when he told me he needed space. I can't take it anymore, but I refuse to let him see the hurt he's causing me.

"Gary, I'm leaving. I don't know what's going on with you, but I'm leaving."

He looks up. I see sadness and a hint of defiance in his brown eyes. I get up and walk out the door. I don't want to be with someone who doesn't want to be with me. Even though my junior and senior years were filled with flirtation between us, once I graduated and we could be together, he lost interest.

I take my pain and confusion and drive home. I want to see my friends but can't right now. What I really want to do is get drunk. I feel dizzy from the emotions of the past six months.

A few days later, I call Mary. She wrote to me while I was in Las Vegas, and I appreciated her staying in touch. Now I don't care who knows about me and Coach Finnegan.

"Are you glad to be home?" she asks me.

"I am. I got to know my birth father and can say that I'm very glad he didn't raise me."

"That bad, huh?"

I tell her about how Don quit talking to me and how I enjoyed being with Joanna. Then I tell her my big secret.

"Listen, there's something I've wanted to tell you about for some time. Coach Finnegan and I dated for a little while this summer."

"You're kidding."

"I'm not. I'd had a crush on him since I had him for economics our junior year. After graduation, I reached out to him because I was crushed I wouldn't see him again."

"What did he say?"

"That he felt the same way about me. Of course, he wanted me to keep our relationship a secret, which I did. Then, right when I thought we were getting more serious, he broke it off."

"Wow. I'm so sorry."

"That's what made me decide to go visit my dad and Joanna—to give Gary space. Unlike you, he didn't write or call. He said he would, but he didn't. I've already been to his new apartment and confronted him. He acted like he doesn't want me around. I feel awful."

# CHAPTER 64

Omicron enters our lives in early January 2022. More than eight hundred thousand people have died since Covid emerged. Mike and I and our close friends remain faithful in wearing our masks. I wear a KN95 mask everywhere I go, feeling safe with it on. And, in addition to our vaccinations, we've had our booster injection.

One day, Mike calls to let me know he is on his way home—he has tested positive for Covid. I'm not the same girl I was when this virus first came out. I trust mask-wearing and that our vaccinations will minimize his body's response to the virus. When he gets home, I greet him at the door.

"I'm sorry," he says. "I've tried to avoid this. I didn't want to bring it home."

"It's okay, honey," I say. "We know what to do. We'll be in each other's arms before you know it. I want you to feel better soon."

"Thanks, babe. I'm going to lie down."

I'm thankful Mike doesn't feel any sicker. I feel like we're old pros at how to handle this situation.

I love him so much. And it's not just me. Mike's patients love him. Our friends love him. I'm so blessed to be married to him.

A few days later, I text Brooke to let her know about Mike. I'm supposed to see her in person in the next ten days. I tell her that he's feeling better, his cough is improving, and I've tested negative so far and haven't had any symptoms. Brooke agrees that sticking with our scheduled meeting the next week should be fine.

I marvel at how far I've come with my fears about Covid. I feel I've been surrounded by love and understanding since the start of it. *Thank You, God.*

# CHAPTER 65

It's December 1980. While I was living in Las Vegas, my stepfather, Tom, married Jackie and now they live in an old farmhouse in Ringgold, Georgia. After Christmas, Dad/Tom calls me.

"Hey, hon," he says. "Jackie and I want to know if you'd be willing to take care of our house while we go away for the weekend. You can invite friends to stay here too."

I feel lost. Mom is dating her childhood boyfriend and I'm about to start college. Gary has left me feeling so confused, I don't know up from down. My parents are lost to each other; Dad/Tom took care of that. Now he wants me to stay at his and his new wife's house. I'm not crazy about the idea, but I agree.

I invite some high school friends to spend the night with me in the white farmhouse that sits in the middle of sparse woods. An abandoned pool lies just beyond the front porch.

On Friday afternoon, the crunch of tires tells me my friends are here. Mary, Debbie, and three other friends arrive at the same time and I welcome them with pleasure.

After they settle their things, we talk and laugh and munch on snacks. I smile and go along with everyone but feel miles away. I tell all of them about Gary and they are stunned.

"I don't believe that you and Coach kissed," Debbie says.

"It's true, but it's over," I say. "I don't know what happened."

I feel flat. Sharing about Gary and me doesn't bring me any relief or happiness. It would have been different if I'd told them in the thick of our relationship.

That night, three of us pile in Dad and Jackie's king-size bed. The others spread out on the floor and couch. I feel weird being in Dad's bed, and sadness weighs on me as I think about the early days with him and Mom. I roll away from my friends and stare at the wall. Tears slide down my face. I've never felt so alone in my life. I stare at the bedside clock. I sense time will move at a snail's pace until morning.

Several weeks later, I start school without any books. Dad/Don said he would help pay for school, but there's a catch: He wants me to send him receipts and *then* he'll send me the money. Don's mad that Mom borrowed $350 from the savings account he set up to help pay for my last semester of high school. How am I supposed to afford both books and tuition? Babysitting for my old neighbor Bozo and his wife Margaret isn't enough, and school takes up too much of my time for a regular job.

One day when I'm babysitting, I share my woes with Bozo and Margaret. As we talk, Bozo, whose real name is John, offers me a lifeline.

"Well, Fish," he says, "my new business is starting to pick up. I could use your help."

"Really? That would be great."

"I agree," Margaret says. "John could use your help at the shop, and I may be able to cut back my hours so I can be home with the children when they get off the bus."

Relief washes over me. I don't know what I'd do without their help. Plus, I've known Bozo since I was a young girl. I trust him.

By February, I'm working enough hours with Bozo to buy the last of my textbooks for the semester. Bozo, Margaret, and I work well together and laugh a lot. I'm getting the hang of the shipping part of the business. The bus drops the children off at the shop and they do their homework in the back. I love getting hugs from them. They beg for me to babysit again.

"I will," I say. "I promise I'll find some time soon."

The next month, Margaret announces that she will cut back her hours soon. I'm glad I'm able to help them and I feel like I belong to a family. The money is so much better than babysitting. They are wonderful people to work for and I'm glad they're in my life. I'm lucky to have had Bozo as my neighbor as a child. He has always supported me. I think I still have his army jacket.

Later in the month, I turn nineteen. Mom is spending all her time with Dan, her boyfriend. I guess she's lonely; I didn't think she would date anyone again. I want her to be happy and she seems to be, but I miss her. I also want to do well in college, so I study hard when I'm not working. My choice now is to succeed and not depend on anyone ever again.

# CHAPTER 66

Margaret begins to work fewer hours. "I think between you and John, the work is getting done," she announces. "I think I can cut back my hours now to do more at home and be available for the boys after school."

I'll miss her but am happy for her.

"And I have projects I want to do that I never have time for," she adds. "I'm really looking forward to getting to them. But don't worry, I'll come in every now and then."

The shop is quieter without her. Margaret has such a sweet personality. I think Bozo made a good decision when he married her.

Business is going well and I'm busy with shipping, grateful for this job. I feel safe, am making decent money, and am thankful to them for my work here.

Several weeks later, while I'm preparing a shipment, Bozo comes behind me and hugs me. "I get wet every time I see you," he whispers.

My heart stops. *No. Please no.* Why me? I don't know what to do. I don't know what to say. I don't want to hurt his feelings, but what about Margaret and his children? I love his family. This behavior is such a betrayal to them.

"You're so beautiful," he says. "You've grown into a foxy woman. Your body is so strong and athletic."

He turns me around and kisses me. My body responds to his, while a pit works its way into my stomach. A part of me feels flattered; I yearn for attention, but not this kind. I struggle to catch my breath. A few minutes pass and he lets me get back to work. His eyes are gleaming. The familiar darkness of shame wraps its tentacles around me.

Each week, Bozo gets bolder. My heart responds to his attention by shutting out how wrong his actions are. I fear being caught, but there's no turning back. I feel like a splatter of dark and light. How will this nightmare end?

One afternoon, he takes me to the back of the shop and eases me onto the couch—the same couch where the children did their homework. The lights are off. *I just want to work.*

"I want to taste you," he says. "Just relax and lie down."

Like a prisoner, I do as I'm told. And like a prisoner, I'm being tortured. I want to get out of myself and leave. He slides my shorts and underwear off. I swear to myself that I won't let him have sexual intercourse with me. Even thinking about that terrifies me. My heart hammers and I feel heat on my face. Bozo approaches me with hooded eyes. I feel so vulnerable and embarrassed. *Hurry up with whatever it is you're going to do.*

His body is hovering over me and his head moves down below my waist. He licks me and moans. "You taste delicious. I want to be the one to teach you about sex. It can be a wonderful thing."

My hands clench. He comes up to my mouth to kiss me. Yuck. I turn my head. I don't want to be a part of this horror. I want to go home and take a shower. How do I get in these circumstances? Pleasing people comes at a high price for me.

Bozo moves back to the workroom. I pull up my underwear and shorts and go into the bathroom. I switch the light on and stare at my defeated face. I hate what he did. I wipe myself, but I smell him on my shirt. I don't know if it's his cologne or his deodorant. I just know it's him.

Five o'clock can't come soon enough. I want out of here and am already dreading tomorrow. *Please, God, don't let it happen again.* This man is not who I thought he was. He took advantage of my love for touch and twisted it to meet his needs. He has taken away my friendship with Margaret and the children. I'm devastated.

# CHAPTER 67

It's the end of January 2022. I sit on my therapist's couch. We take our masks off. A floor fan swirls the air. We meet each other's eyes and smile.

"Steph," Brooke says. "I need to tell you something before we get started."

"You're moving," I say.

Her eyes widen. "You're the second person I've told," she says.

"You said something a few months back that made me think you might move soon. I'm happy for you. Are you moving closer to your grandson?"

"We are. But I want you to know that I will be available to you through teletherapy after we move."

"You know, Brooke," I say, with a laugh, "If you had announced your move a few years ago, I'd probably be on the floor holding onto your ankle."

"I know you would. It's one of the reasons the timing feels right. You've worked hard on yourself and have come a long way."

"Your guidance is immeasurable. I know I've done the work, but your walking with me has helped me through it all."

We look at each other and smile. I then tell her I'm almost finished with the first draft of my book and writing about my experience with Bozo.

"When I get to these parts of the book, the super hard ones, I remind myself that I survived. Even though I have to go through the memories of the experiences, I know now that I have a voice—something I lacked at the time."

"You were wanting to be a part of a family. You trusted him, but he betrayed you. He ruined your relationship with his wife too. He put you in a no-win situation. And, as a teenager, it's hard to stand up to those who are older or are in authority. Your parents were divorced and involved in their relationships. Your need to be liked was also paramount to you at that time. You were confused and vulnerable and he took advantage of that."

Brooke's kind eyes look through me—at least that's what if feels like.

"I enjoy writing, but this memoir thing is hard. Maybe I'll write fiction next time."

We laugh.

"Stephanie, what do you think Mike had that everyone else didn't?"

"I believe he was a gift from God. I know that sounds silly, but I felt safe with him right off the bat. I know I felt that way and was wrong many times before. But with Mike, there was a kindness and depth to him that felt new and refreshing. Every time I try to peg him as being one way or another, he surprises me. He's funny and unpredictable. When we were first dating, we could be dressed to the nines on our way to some residents' function but, if a creek or river were nearby, Mike would pull over to see if there were any salamanders under rocks. If a live snake were in the road, he would pull it off and move it to safety. That goes for about any animal. Life matters to him. Soon after we married, I woke up one morning to find that he had landscaped our yard during the night. Who does that?"

Brooke smiles and leans forward in her chair. Our time is up.

# CHAPTER 68

"I need your help at a show in Gatlinburg next weekend," Bozo says. "Margaret can't come."

It's April 1981. I'm nineteen years old.

"We'll have to spend the night," he continues. "I need to call on a client the night before the show, but I'll pay you for your time and take care of everything."

A coldness fills my body even though it's April and in the 70s. Will we have separate rooms? I don't think so.

"Can we stop off in Knoxville at UT's campus on our way? I'd like to visit one of my friends. Debbie's a student there."

"Sure," he answers. "It's on the way."

Bozo's hunger for me seems to grow by the day. His need for oral sex makes me feel awful even when my body betrays me. He hasn't tried intercourse yet, but I won't let that happen. Guilt would seep into my bones, and there's no part of me ready for it. I don't want to lose my virginity to him or anyone else right now—nor do I want to risk getting pregnant. I'd prefer being married to the one I want to spend my life with before bringing a child into the world. The only choice I feel I have right now is not to hurt his feelings—as long as his sexual fantasies go no further. I don't know what else to do.

Next weekend comes fast. Bozo has been whistling at work all week and I'm looking forward to seeing Debbie. We load up his old van with supplies. Smells of oil and dust float through the open windows from inside the vehicle. Farms fly by as we make our way northward in eastern Tennessee. This trip will be my first visit to the University of Tennessee's Knoxville campus.

All I think about is seeing Debbie. Otherwise, my stomach turns sour. Bozo smiles all the way there. When we get to the campus, he drops me off at our meeting spot and says he'll be back in an hour to pick me up.

As I hop out of the van, I see Debbie walking my way. Our timing is perfect. We hug. She asks me if I want a quick tour of the school.

I look up at the tall buildings and sprawling campus. It's so much bigger than mine. I'm happy to be with her, feeling so much better. This outing is normal—two college friends visiting each other. Normal will disappear the second I climb back into the van with Bozo.

While we're walking, Debbie asks me why I'm going to Gatlinburg. I hate to lie. Even if I tell her a partial truth, it will still be dishonest.

"I'm helping my boss. He has a meeting with a client and a trade show."

I feel awful, so I change the subject.

I listen to Debbie talk about her first year. I'm happy for her.

Our hour is over before I'm ready. I dread leaving her. I want to tell Debbie what's going on and have her help me out of this mess, but shame keeps my lips closed. She walks me to Bozo's van and I introduce them. I get in the van and we pull away.

I don't feel like talking. My head begins to throb and I feel sad.

An hour or so later, we pull into the hotel's parking lot. Bozo whistles while he carries our bags and unlocks one door. My heart sinks. I guess I'm sleeping in the same room with him.

"Come on in, come in," he says to usher me in from outside.

"Is there just one bed?" I ask.

"Yes, but it's king-size."

"Oh."

He sets the bags down and looks at me. "I'm going to take a shower," he says. "Want to join me?"

"No."

"Come on, it'll be fun."

"No. I'm not dirty."

"I could wash you and you could wash me."

"That's okay."

I don't want to see him naked. He does his best to strip in front of me. I pretend to check out the hotel room. What have I gotten myself into? I thought I knew this man. After he kissed me on the lips, all that changed. He isn't who I thought he was.

I hear the shower turn off. Bozo struts out of the bathroom, but I look away. He hops in the bed and pats the other side.

"Come lie down. Take off your clothes."

My heart hammers. I feel my chest tighten. *This is not going to happen.*

"I want to teach you about sex," he says. "You want to enjoy it and it takes practice. I want to be your teacher."

"I don't want to take off my clothes." *And you aren't going to be my teacher.*

He sighs and looks away. "Okay, then. Come lie beside me."

I feel stiff as I sit on the bed. He reaches for me and pulls me behind him. My head feels like it's going to burst.

"Let me have your hand." He places it on his penis. He shows me how to rub him, but I don't meet his standards. He rubs himself and comes. I look away.

My headache begins to ease. I'm proud of myself for standing up to him. I found my voice this time. I said no to taking a shower with him and no about taking off my clothes. I chose my own needs over his. I don't like disappointing people, but I have *some* limits. I want to learn how to stand up for myself more often—even when the issue isn't as important.

That night, I wear my pajamas and stay to the other side of the bed, wrapping another blanket I found in the closet tight around myself. He doesn't make any more moves. It's like my saying no broke a spell. I fall asleep to the rattle of the air conditioner.

The rest of the weekend is a blur. Bozo frowns while he carries out his business and I'm surprised that I don't feel the need to make him happy. Instead, anger worms its way into my heart. He has ruined our relationship, as well as mine with his family's.

A few weeks later, I'm let go. He tells me that business is slow, but he doesn't look at me when he says it. Free of him, I feel a sense of relief. And I carry the guilt of not having said no to him in the beginning. I make room in the secret space in my heart and tuck away my remorse.

# CHAPTER 69

It's the end of September 1981. Life gives me many opportunities to learn to say no. There are times I keep my boundaries and times I let them slip. After I'm fired from my job with Bozo, his brother offers me a job at his shop. The business is kept locked and looks insignificant from the outside.

There are rows and rows of merchandise. The man chases me around the shop and tries to kiss me throughout the day.

I hear him chuckle. "Where are you?" he calls. He sees me and runs at me, but I run away before he can pinch me.

"Stop," I say. "I'm trying to work." I don't like this man at all.

The brothers have different approaches, but I decide both are sex crazed. They don't care about me. They just want to exploit me.

One day, I show a customer a multi-blade knife. He must be a special customer since he is allowed inside the building. The six-inch blade pops into place. The next blade slips from my fingers and comes down across my left pointer finger at the knuckle.

I'm afraid to look down. I'm sure my finger is sliced in half, but it isn't. The client yells for my boss, who tells me to sit down until I'm able to drive myself to the emergency room. I'm given a wet paper towel to staunch the bleeding.

No questions about my safety or offers to drive me to the ER. No concern. Instead, my boss says, "Try not to bleed on the rug." I work another month more and then quit.

In another relationship, I try to have romantic feelings, but they aren't there. We are best friends and that is all I can give him. I know I confuse him by wanting to spend a lot of time with him.

After a few years, I'm able to say no to further attempts to engage in an amorous way. Even though I don't like hurting people, I stand my ground.

It's 1983. I call my friend from Happening #5, Will Kidd. We did missionary work with Episcopal youth from across Tennessee in Costa Rica during the summer of 1981.

I tell Will I've figured something out. "When you're young you don't have much money, but you are in the best physical shape. When you're older and have money, you might not be in good health to travel."

"Yeah, that's true."

"I want to travel. I've never been to DC or New York City or Canada. Want to join me?"

"Yeah, man. Let's do it."

I scrape up $364 and borrow my brother's old pup tent. Before we hit the road together, we make some rules. Rule number 1: Nothing sexual.

Even though we sleep a few inches apart, I feel alone. I don't try to make any moves, but neither does he. *What's the matter with me? Am I not cute enough for him?*

Long after our adventures, we write each other about what happened between us. Or, more precisely, what didn't happen.

"I'm not sure what happened," Will writes. "I know I withheld things that we should have talked about. I lacked the courage and longing it takes to really give myself to someone. I attribute a lot of that to the immensity of what we were doing: new environments, four thousand miles, bad nutrition, hotel rooms, flooded tent, fatigue, poor quality rest. Hell, it was hard enough to survive, let alone going on to meet all our emotional and spiritual needs."

Two years later, I become a nurse. I'm working second shift as a pediatric nurse. My creed is not to date a doctor. I don't want that lifestyle. My uncle is an obstetrician/gynecologist. He works one hundred plus hours per week. My birth father is an anesthesiologist. His practice is more important to him than his children.

I say no to the training physicians who ask me out. Instead, I say yes to the chief of the residents. A doctor. What am I thinking? My resolve dissipates immediately.

"Do you want me to teach you about photography?" asks Nathan.

This doctor is cute and important. He manages the pediatric intensive care unit and the residency program. He's a good physician and is at least fourteen years older than I am.

"Yes," I say. "I love to take pictures, but I don't have a decent camera."

"I have one you can use. Are you off this weekend?"

"I am."

"Let's meet at Reflection Riding. Do you know where it is?"

"No, but I've heard of it."

While Nathan gives me directions, my heart skips a beat. I hear he lives in an apartment and that he and his wife are divorced.

After that day, Nathan and I spend as much time together as we can. He brings me to his apartment, where we talk photography and make out. One night, during my three to eleven shift, Nathan comes by the nurse's station and pulls me aside.

"Do you want to spend the night after you get off work?" he asks.

"Yes. I'll run home and grab some clothes and then join you."

He has a pullout bed that takes up a portion of the den. The one bedroom is kept for when his daughter visits him.

Nathan starts to undress, and I follow his lead.

"Come sit beside me," he says and pats the bed. "Have you ever had intercourse?"

I feel my face heat up. I turn away from him, feeling like a child.

"Hey, it's okay. I'll be gentle."

He brings me to him and begins kissing my face and neck. I feel warm all over. He slides a condom on and eases into me. It hurts some, but then begins to feel good. I want more.

Afterward, he says, "You're going to be sore and may have scant bleeding. Let me know if you do and I'll get something for you."

He gets up and passes gas as he heads to the bathroom.

Oh my gosh. I can't believe I had sex. What a difference it makes to be with the one you want to be with. I appreciate Nathan's sensitivity to my being a virgin—at twenty-five.

His ex-wife calls one morning as we are eating breakfast. Their daughter has run away. I ask him about his family. During the conversation, I learn a hard fact.

"Well, technically, we're still married. We've been separated for three months."

"You aren't divorced?"

"No, but we are heading in that direction."

"I need to leave."

*I can't believe I've committed adultery. The very thing I can't stand.* Both of Mom's husbands had affairs. I don't have time for that. I won't do it.

I need to clear my head. A week or so later, I fly to Hawaii to meet my mom and her husband, Dan, on their vacation, then stop in Las Vegas for a short visit with Don and Joanna on my way home. Nathan wants to know if he can pick me up at the airport.

"No. I can't see you. You are *married*!"

After I return, we meet one last time in a shopping mall parking lot.

"Aren't we going to get married?" he asks.

I flick some dirt off his car fender and take a deep breath.

"No, we aren't."

As we part, he reminds me that I'm his ingénue. I ask him what it means.

"Look it up," he replies.

I'm sad. Our relationship feels like a tragedy in a play. He is going through a midlife crisis and my looking up to him was never going to work. I think my desire to be noticed has to do with my need to connect with important, older people. It's these people I hustle for love.

Later, I look up the definition of *ingenue*: "An innocent or unsophisticated young woman." I'm not sure if he's insulting me or feeling that he took advantage of me. Perhaps he means both.

# CHAPTER 70

It's the end of February 2022 and finally Covid-19 infection rates are dropping. Mike and I sit on our love seat and watch the news. The CDC announces that masks are no longer needed indoors, both for the vaccinated and unvaccinated.

"I think that's a mistake," I say. "I'm not ready to give up wearing my KN95 mask."

"Me neither."

"There are still too many Americans who are not vaccinated. I'll feel better when I get my second booster in April."

Mike nods. "I'm full of antibodies since I had Covid last month."

"I'm not feeling afraid so much as I don't want to deal with the potential long-term side effects."

Mike reaches for my hand.

"You know," he says, "we have our thirty-second anniversary coming up in May."

"I can't believe it. I'm so glad we met when we did."

"It's all about timing. If we'd met during high school, you wouldn't have paid any attention to me."

"We wouldn't have been in the same crowds, that's for sure. You were a much more virtuous person than I was."

"You were too cool for me."

"It's not too late to grow out your hair and wear an earring—although your dad would haunt me for that."

"He just might. Besides, I like my hair the way it is."

"What about the earring?"

We laugh and kiss.

# CHAPTER 71

After Mike and I eat at the restaurant that evening in 1989, I want to be with him every minute of every day and I want to be my best with him. Mike feels the same way. I can't believe I'm falling for him. I have a trip around the world waiting for me. Maybe he'll still be interested when I return.

Five weeks later, I'm in my office getting ready for the day. It's 6:00 a.m. I rub my eyes and try to focus on my paperwork. I open my mouth wide and yawn as I stretch out my arms over my head. Mike knocks on my door.

When I open the door, the blinds bang against the window as he rushes in. He kisses me and then takes a step back. He drops his hazel eyes for a second, then looks me straight in the eye.

"I just have to ask you something. It can't wait."

I feel my heart pick up its beat. What is he going to ask?

The words rush out. "Will you marry me? I know we've only dated five weeks . . ."

My mind races to images of world travel and then back to his proposal. I'll take him over any trip. "Yes!"

He pulls me into him and kisses me.

"I don't have a ring or anything . . ."

"That's fine. I don't need one."

"Can we get married in March?"

"That's only three months away. I've been in a lot of weddings. They take a lot to plan, and I want a big wedding. How about May?"

"That's great!"

I can't believe it. I'm so happy. I love this man. We get along so well. I'm not keen on his being a doctor, but I'm marrying Mike Maley, who just happens to be a doctor.

"I've got to call my mom," I say. "She's going to be so happy! She already loves you to pieces."

"I love her too. I'm so happy you said yes."

"Thank you for asking me!"

I pick up the phone and call Mom.

"Hey, honey. What's going on? Aren't you at work?"

"Mike asked me to marry him!" My voice cracks and tears stream down my face. Mike holds my hand and smiles.

Mom is ecstatic. "You're making me cry and messing up my makeup. I'm so happy for you. He's a wonderful person."

When we hang up, I look at my watch. Mike sees the time. We kiss and rush to our work.

I burst into the newborn nursery. "Guess what?"

The other nurses and nursing assistants stop what they're doing and look at me.

"Mike proposed to me! I said yes!"

They rush me with hugs and smiles. In the next moment, we hear the doorbell that sounds just like the one in the Avon commercials. We hurry to prepare for a newborn heading our way from labor and delivery. I feel light and new. I feel safe and loved enough that someone wants to spend their life with me. I know I want to spend mine with him.

# CHAPTER 72

It's June 2022—my favorite time of year. I shower and stretch and head to the kitchen. I bend over to pick up Mike's love note for today.

"Good morning, Steph! I wonder what new challenges this day will bring. Whatever it is, I know I will be okay because I have you in my life. I love you. Mike."

In our other home, I decorated our kitchen cabinets with the rainbow-colored notes. Now I use one of the timber frame posts in our main room. The notes don't stick as well on the post, but it doesn't matter. His words stay with me throughout the day.

Even after thirty-two years, our love for each other continues to build. Every few years on our anniversary, Mike and I write our five-year goals on scraps of paper.

In 2020, we wrote the same first two goals:

"Living in our new home on Lake Hartwell," Mike wrote. "Have traveled around the world more . . ."

"Living on the lake in a sustainable house (including bees, solar panels, rainwater collection). World travel . . ." I wrote.

We first did this exercise when we were doing premarital counseling with Dr. Curtis, the priest who arrived at our church when I was still in high school. He introduced us to this practice, and Mike and I have kept up the discipline. It amazes us how our goals mimic or overlap each other.

The other weekend, I sat inside, reading a book. Mike was piddling outside. I headed outdoors to find him.

"Hey, babe," I said. "Thanks for blowing off the driveway. It looks nice. When are you going to be finished working out here?"

"I can stop right now. Wanna take a walk?"

"Yes. I need some Mike time and to move my body."

He set down the electric weed eater and reached for my hand.

We are getting better at asking for what we want. Our faith keeps us strong and is the glue to our relationship. Communication is close behind.

I have not written my funeral plans. My fear of the virus plummeted with the advent of vaccinations and protective masks. Writing my way through present fears and past vulnerabilities filled my dark spaces with light and love. *Thank You, God.*

Writing this story has released me from shame and guilt. I'm free—I'm no longer the girl who is a victim to predators. My secrets are released. I have let them go.

Today, my life is abundant. Lake water surrounds our home. Deer and rabbits inhabit our property. Family and friends find a haven here. I prefer being here more than anywhere else. Our sons are happy and healthy. Mike and I feel such gratitude.

I think about our conversation last week. "I still can't believe we get to live here," I told him.

"Me neither. I'm so glad we bought both pieces of property. The view is unbelievable."

We hug.

Healing takes time. It requires intention. With God's help, the young girl in me, and the woman I am today, are whole. This journey has not been easy, but well worth it. My heart leans into love and kindness and peace.

Mike and I join each other on our back deck. We sit together, hold hands, and watch the play of light on the water as the sun goes down.

# ACKNOWLEDGMENTS

Laura Munson, my professional editor, believed in me when I first called her in 2013 to attend one of her Haven Retreats. "I'm not a writer," I said; "Come join us," Laura said. Without your help and support, I wouldn't be where I am today. Your gift of creating a safe place has been huge. Thank you seems insufficient. I must also include a thank you to my Haven alums and Haven writing group. You inspire me.

I want to thank my line editor, Billy Chism, for sticking with me through it all. He never wavered in his professionalism. He didn't blink an eye at the tough parts. My sentence structure is so much better because of him.

And thanks to my early listeners: Joanna Salmon, Mike Maley, Cindy Bowers, and Edith Swarthout.

And to my Steph's Writings Newsletter readers. Your time and comments mean the world to me.

And to those of you who read my book and wrote a blurb for it. Picture me with my hand on my heart. Your keen attention grabbed my own. Thank you.

BIG thank-you to Brooke Warner for saying *yes* to my book. I've never appreciated a green light so much as the one she gave me. The team at She Writes Press has felt more like a family than a business. To my proofreaders Jill Angel and Ann Marie Jackson—your ideas made my book even better. I appreciate your comments of support too. To Megan Milton, thank you for your patience and calm presence as my project manager. I needed both in abundance.

An unexpected gift throughout the publishing process was meeting so many other authors—especially the ones in the Fall 2025 cohort group. I learned about grace and how to flow with the book publishing process. I especially want to thank our cohort leaders, Barbara Stark-Nemon and Leslie Johansen Nack, for being just that—leaders (and encouragers).

To my Good Vibrations women's group: You know how to love and support. I feel you every step of the way. Thank you for your authenticity. Eighteen years and still sending out good vibes.

To the people throughout my life who helped me along the way—especially during my first nineteen years: You are the ones who balanced me and taught me about another way to live.

And thank you to my family and my chosen family. You love me unconditionally, sustain me, and cheer me on. This includes my best friend, who wrote the incredible poem at the beginning of my book, and her daughters, who are like my own. I will never be the same without our T.

To my husband, Mike, who made me the luckiest girl in the world when he asked me to marry him: I love you with all that I have. And finally, to our sons: You show me new ways to think about the world as you light up mine.

# ABOUT THE AUTHOR

Author photo © Steph Maley

**Stephanie L. Maley,** *a native of Chattanooga, Tennessee, dreamed of writing a book since she was a young woman. Thirty years later, that dream found its way to a reality. Before becoming an author, Stephanie worked as a pediatric nurse after getting her BSN, home-educated her two sons, and became a professional photographer after obtaining an associate's degree in photography at forty-eight years old (www.lov2shoot.com). She and her husband, Mike, live in their dream home on Lake Hartwell in Northeast, Georgia, where you can find Steph swimming, paddleboarding, kayaking, and driving her boat.*

## **Looking for your next great read?**

We can help!

Visit www.shewritespress.com/next-read
or scan the QR code below for a list
of our recommended titles.

She Writes Press is an award-winning
independent publishing company founded to
serve women writers everywhere.